BIBLE

Dr. Victor Paul Furnish is University Distinguished Professor of New Testament in Southern Methodist University's Perkins School of Theology, where he has served on the faculty since 1959. Dr. Furnish has earned degrees from Cornell College of Iowa, Garrett-Evangelical Theological Seminary, and Yale University. Author of many scholarly works, among them *Theology and Ethics in Paul* (1968; Korean translation, 1982), Dr. Furnish is General Editor of the Abingdon New Testament commentaries, a twenty-volume series now in preparation. Dr. Furnish is an ordained minister of The United Methodist Church.

JOURNEY THROUGH THE BIBLE: ROMANS, 1 CORINTHIANS, 2 CORINTHIANS, GALATIANS, EPHESIANS, PHILIPPIANS. An official resource for The United Methodist Church prepared by the General Board of Discipleship through Church School Publications and published by Cokesbury, The United Methodist Publishing House; 201 Eighth Avenue, South; P.O. Box 801; Nashville, TN 37202-0801. Printed in the United States of America. Copyright ©1995 by Cokesbury. All rights reserved.

Scripture quotations in this publication, unless otherwise indicated, are from the New Revised Standard Version of the Bible, copyright ©1989 by the Division of Christian Education of the National Council of the Churches of Christ in the United States of America, and are used by permission. All rights reserved.

For permission to reproduce any material in this publication, call 615-749-6421, or write to Permissions Office, P.O. Box 801, Nashville, TN 37202.

To order copies of this publication, call toll free 800-672-1789. Call Monday–Friday 7:00–6:30 Central Time or 5:00–4:30 Pacific Time; Saturday, 9:00–5:00. Use your Cokesbury account, American Express, Visa, Discover, or MasterCard.

EDITORIAL TEAM
Debra G. Ball-Kilbourne,
    Editor
Linda H. Leach,
    Assistant Editor
Linda O. Spicer,
    Adult Section Assistant

DESIGN TEAM
Teresa B. Travelstead,
    Layout Designer
Susan J. Scruggs, Design
    Supervisor, Cover Design

ADMINISTRATIVE STAFF
Neil M. Alexander,
    Vice-President, Publishing
Duane A. Ewers,
    Editor of Church School
    Publications
Gary L. Ball-Kilbourne,
    Senior Editor of Adult
    Publications

 Cokesbury

Photos: © Biblical Archaeology Society. Used by permission.

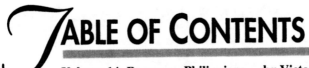
TABLE OF CONTENTS

Volume 14: Romans—Philippians   by Victor Paul Furnish

2		INTRODUCTION TO THE SERIES
3	Chapter 1	BEING HUMAN
11	Chapter 2	A VISION OF FREEDOM
19	Chapter 3	CHRISTIANS AND JEWS
28	Chapter 4	DISCOVERING WHAT IS GOOD
37	Chapter 5	STRANGE WISDOM
45	Chapter 6	PARTICULAR GIFTS
53	Chapter 7	NECESSARY KNOWLEDGE
61	Chapter 8	FAITH, INCORPORATED
69	Chapter 9	A NEW CREATION
77	Chapter 10	STRENGTH THROUGH WEAKNESS
85	Chapter 11	CHILDREN OF PROMISE
93	Chapter 12	ONE NEW HUMANITY
101	Chapter 13	ONE NAME ABOVE ALL
109		PAUL'S LIFE AND LETTERS: A CHRONOLOGY
110		PAUL'S LIFE AND MINISTRY
112		PAUL AND THE CORINTHIANS, A.D. 50-57
Inside back cover		MAP: THE WORLD OF PAUL

11 12 13 - 19 18

$\mathcal{J}$NTRODUCTION TO THE SERIES

Welcome to JOURNEY THROUGH THE BIBLE!!
You are about to embark on an adventure that can change your life.

WHAT TO BRING WITH YOU
Don't worry about packing much for your trip. All you need to bring with you on this journey are
- an openness to God speaking to you in the words of Scripture
- companions to join you on the way, and
- your Bible

ITINERARY
In each session of this volume of JOURNEY THROUGH THE BIBLE, first you will be offered some hints for what to look for as you read the Bible text, and then you will be guided through four "dimensions" of study. Each is intended to help you through a well-rounded appreciation and application of the Bible's words.

HOW TO PREPARE FOR YOUR JOURNEY THROUGH THE BIBLE
Although you will gain much if all you do is show up for Bible study and participate willingly in the session, you can do a few things to gain even more:
- Read in advance the Bible passage mentioned in What to Watch For, using the summaries and hints as you read.
- During your Bible reading, answer the questions in Dimension 1.
- Read the rest of the session in this study book.
- Try a daily discipline of reading the Bible passages suggested in Dimension 4. Note that the Bible texts listed in Dimension 4 do *not* relate to a particular session. But if you continue with this daily discipline, by the end of thirteen weeks, you will have read through *all* of that portion of the Bible covered by this volume.

Studying the Bible is a lifelong project. JOURNEY THROUGH THE BIBLE provides you with a guided tour for a few of the steps along your way. May God be with you on your journey!

Gary L. Ball-Kilbourne
Senior Editor, Adult Publications
Church School Publications

Questions or comments?
Call Curric-U-Phone 1-800-251-8591

BEING HUMAN

What to Watch For

The focus passage for this session is Romans 3:21–4:25. In an opening paragraph Paul summarized several of his most basic beliefs. Next he responded to certain objections that he supposed people might raise with reference to what he had said. In the remainder of the passage the apostle illustrated some of his main points by drawing on a story from the church's Scripture.

The following affirmations in these paragraphs are worth special attention:
➤ Before God, all human beings are equal.
➤ Righteousness cannot be gained through the law, but comes only as a gift from God.
➤ This gift of righteousness is known through Jesus Christ, who died for us and was raised up by God.
➤ In the Old Testament story of Abraham and Sarah, we can see that the gift of righteousness is to be received by faith on the basis of God's promise.
➤ Faith requires acknowledging our dependence upon God for life, trusting absolutely in God's promise to sustain and renew us in life.

Dimension 1:
What Does the Bible Say?

1. In what connection did Paul use the word *gift*?

2. When and why was Abraham circumcised?

3. What does the law bring?

4. What specifically did God promise Abraham and Sarah?

Dimension 2:
What Does the Bible Mean?

Paul's Last Surviving Letter

This is perhaps the last surviving letter written by Paul himself, having been dispatched from Corinth probably in A.D. 56 or 57. It is also the apostle's most comprehensive and important statement of his understanding of the gospel. In advance of his first visit to Rome, and because he hoped that the Roman Christians would support his projected mission to Spain, he wanted to introduce them to the basic themes of his preaching (Romans 1:11-15; 15:23-24). He was also intent on addressing some matters that he understood to be at issue between the Jewish-Christian and Gentile-Christian members of the Roman church, matters that were threatening to divide it (14:1–15:13). A third important topic in this letter is how the gospel of Christ is related to God's promises to and purposes for the Jews. This matter was an especially timely one for Paul, because he was about to sail for Jerusalem with an offering for the Christians there (15:25-27), and he was unsure how this gift, contributed by his predominantly Gentile congregations, would be received and might be interpreted (15:30-32).

4

AN OUTLINE OF ROMANS 1–5

Letter opening	1:1-7
Thanksgiving	1:8-15
Thematic statement	1:16-17
The revealing of God's wrath	1:18–3:20
Introduction	1:18-19
Sin's power in the Gentile world	1:20-32
God's impartiality	2:1-16
Sin's power among the Jews	2:17–3:20
The revealing of God's righteousness	3:21–5:21
Righteousness as a gift	3:21–4:25
God's reconciling love in Christ	5:1-11
Christ and Adam	5:12-21

The Saving Power of the Gospel

In order to appreciate what Paul is saying in Romans 3:21–4:25, it is important to note both the thematic statement that opens the main part of this letter (1:16-17) and the section immediately following it (1:18–3:20). In his introductory statement, Paul identified "the gospel" as God's saving power (1:16). It is not just some message about God's power, but the actual saving event itself to be received by faith. Central to this event is the revealing of God's "righteousness" (1:17). Paul's Greek word could also, and perhaps better, be translated as "justice." Righteousness, or justice, is something much more than a "personal attribute" of God. It refers to God's acting justly and establishing just relationships.

Paul wrote first about "the dark side" of God's righteousness, its disclosure as "wrath." He was not thinking of God as "angry" and vengeful, but of God's principled opposition to evil. Evil always experiences God's justice as judgment. More specifically, Paul mentioned the judgment that is visited upon the "ungodliness" and "wickedness" of those who "suppress the truth" (1:18). This reference is a comment about humanity as a whole. No particular individuals or categories of people are in view.

By "the truth" Paul meant the truth about God, which always involves the truth about ourselves as human beings. It is the truth that nothing we call "real," including our own existence, has come into being of itself. To use more traditional religious language, it is the truth that all things are created by God. It is, therefore, also the truth that being human means to be dependent, in the most absolute sense imaginable, upon the One from whom all things have come as a gift. According to Paul, humanity's proper response to this truth is to "honor" the Giver as God (literally, to "glori-

5

fy" God) and to give thanks to God (1:21). Instead, humankind—being human—seizes the gift without acknowledging the Giver, and seeks presumptuously to define life on its own terms. This act is idolatry, confusing ourselves, God's creatures, with God the Creator.

A Futile Attempt to Be Independent

When Paul wrote about the sinfulness of humanity, he meant humanity's striving for independence. *Sin* is humanity's turning away from God in an ultimately futile attempt to be independent of the One from whom it draws its life. When this happens, he believed, all other relationships lose their meaning and begin to break down. "Murphy's Law" is validated: everything that can go wrong does go wrong. Life begins to drain away. Paul offers various examples beginning in Romans 1:22, but these are only incidental to the apostle's main point. Being human means, by definition, both to be other than God and inclined to act as if this intention were not the case.

> The story of Adam in the Garden of Eden, to which Paul referred in Romans 5:12-21, is the story of all humankind. By trying to become more and more like God (sin), Adam spurned the Giver and perverted the precious gift of his own humanity.

This universal human predicament is summarized by Paul at the beginning of our focus passage. Without exception ("there is no distinction"), all human beings "have sinned and fall short of the glory of God" (3:22b-23). Humanity has not sinned by failing to be "like God." Humanity sins by *trying* to be like God; and in this trying it risks the loss of its own true identity as God's creation.

The "Bright Side" of God's Righteousness

Paul's comments about the human condition, however, are only preliminary to what he said about the "bright side" of God's righteousness. Beginning in Romans 3:21, he unfolded the good news that there is deliverance from the ultimately destructive power of sin. Although humanity seeks to abandon God, thereby encountering God's righteousness as wrath, God does not abandon humanity. Through Jesus Christ, God's righteousness is encountered as "grace" (3:21-22a, 24-26).

In Romans 3:24-25 Paul probably made use of an early creedal affirmation, perhaps one with which his readers were familiar. From his additions to this creed, and also from the context in Romans, it is clear what he wanted to emphasize. The righteousness disclosed in Jesus Christ is bestowed "as a gift" (3:24) upon "all who believe" (3:22). As elsewhere in Paul's letters, and throughout much of the Bible, "righteousness" refers primarily to being rightly related to something or someone. The alternate translation, "justice," helps us to remember this, and also to recognize that the verb *justify* (3:23, 26, 28) has the same reference. To be "justified" means to be put into proper alignment—Paul meant, with God. He viewed this as a saving relationship because it is a "re-humanizing" one. Through Christ, humanity is reclaimed for God and restored to its proper place as and within God's creation.

In Romans 3:27-31, following up an earlier remark (3:21), Paul contrasted the righteousness that is given through faith in Jesus Christ with what the law provides.

PAUL AND THE LAW

When Paul referred to "the law," he usually meant, especially, the commandments that are found in the first five books of the Bible, revered by the Jews as the Torah (God's "instruction" mediated through Moses). As a Pharisee, Paul had been utterly devoted to keeping the law. As a Christian, although he still wanted to uphold it (3:31), he no longer regarded it as definitive, either for understanding God or for knowing what God requires.

Paul Turned to Abraham and Sarah

As presented in the present passage, this contrast involves two basic points.

- Since the law is about "works" (3:27-28) and since works depend on one's will and ability to do them, the law can offer no way out of the human predicament. The law cannot exclude the "boasting" that inheres in humanity's turning from God. However, "the law of faith" (3:27) is about God's saving work in reaching out through Christ to rescue humanity from itself (3:24-26; 4:24-25).
- The law is about God's purposes for the Jews and their obligations as God's covenant people. If God is truly "one," then God's purposes must embrace the whole of humankind, Gentiles no less than Jews (3:29-30). Here again, in comparison with Christ the law is found wanting. In and through Christ God's grace is extended to all who have faith, whether they are Gentiles or Jews (3:20).

In order to show what faith is, Paul turned to the story in Genesis about Abraham and Sarah (4:1-25). According to the apostle's interpretation of Genesis 15:6 (which he quoted in 4:3), Abraham's righteousness was given ("reckoned") to him on the basis of his believing God, not because he had succeeded in doing certain necessary works of the law (4:1-5, 9, 22). What Abraham "believed" was God's promise of life—that despite their extreme old age, he and Sarah would be blessed by offspring (4:16-18).

Paul emphasized two points, especially, about Abraham's faith.

- It required giving up the illusion that he and Sarah could of themselves generate life; his own body "was already as good as dead," and Sarah's womb was barren (4:19).
- It meant trusting absolutely in the promise of God, whom Abraham honored as the Creator of all that exists and the One who gives life to the dead (4:17). By thus acknowledging that life comes only as a gift, Abraham was giving God the glory (4:20), and thereby already experiencing the renewal of his own life.

Dimension 3:
What Does the Bible Mean to Us?

Making a Difference in the Way We Live

Paul devoted the first eleven chapters of Romans to matters of fundamental theological importance, reserving his most practical counsels and directives for the closing chapters of the letter. Yet the earlier chapters are by no means removed from everyday life. All of Paul's letters, including this one, were written during the course of his exhausting and often dangerous apostolic labors, and were addressed to congregations that stood in constant and sometimes urgent need of pastoral support and direction. Therefore, even where Paul himself did not draw out the practical implications of his thought, attentive readers will be able to do that in ways that are specifically meaningful for them.

Paul's discussion of righteousness, faith, and the law in Romans 3:21–4:25, along with the understanding of being human that his discussion presupposed, invites reflection on several matters that could make a difference in the way we live.

This passage reminds us that life is not in any ultimate sense at our own disposal. The old tale of Abraham and Sarah is a compelling metaphor for the human condition. We may manipulate life in various ways, of course, sometimes for good, sometimes not. But even such astounding feats of medical technology as *in vitro* fertilization, organ transplantation, and artificial respiration amount only to a kind of tinkering, as compared with the actual creation of life itself. Being human means being the recipient of the precious gift of life. None of the differences that distinguish and sometimes divide the world's peoples—whether sexual, ethnic, cultural, social, political, or religious—are as definitive of their existence as this gift of life that unites them as one.

A Reflection on the Meaning of Sin

Our passage also prompts reflection on the meaning of sin. Since being human means not being God, the possibility for sin (denying our dependence on God) is a given of creation itself. The issue is whether we will recognize and accept our humanity, and the frailties and limitations that go along with it. The sorry alternative is to be consumed by a sense of self-importance and invincibility that is dehumanizing both to oneself and to others.

It is not uncommon to hear a person with some terminal illness say that she or he has experienced, for the very first time, what it means really to live. What accounts for this paradox? The answer seems clear. Accepting the reality of our own mortality is the first step toward accepting the truth of our being human, and thereby experiencing the truth that we owe our existence to Another. Similarly, so long as we deny our mortality, and therefore the truth about our humanity, we are also denying the truth about God. This dehumanizing of ourselves leads to a dehumanizing of our relationships with others, as we seek to control and exploit them in accord with our own ambitions. With this effort, their humanity, too, has been diminished, and God's whole creation is put at risk.

"Getting It Right"

This passage, however, is less about sin and the loss of our humanity than it is about "getting it right"—that is, about righteousness and our flourishing as human beings. Righteousness, as Paul conceived it, is not simply the product of human moral efforts. It is the relationship that exists between God and humanity by reason of God's being God.

Trusting in God means giving up the illusion that we are able, of ourselves, either to generate life, to "get it right," or to endow it with meaning. For example, trusting God requires abandoning the notion that "getting it right" and flourishing as an individual, a family, or a nation, depends on

> For those who trust in God, "getting it right" is always experienced, like life itself, as an unconditional gift.

achieving some particular level of wealth, power, or honor. These are not intrinsically evil, but neither are they intrinsically good. To pursue them as if they were intrinsically good, as ends in themselves, is to fall into idolatry. With this pursuit, we experience alienation from both God and our own essential identity as God's creation. Eventually, we are also estranged from others, as we come to regard them either as means or as obstacles to our quest for still greater wealth, power, or honor.

Trusting in God also requires our abandoning the notion that "getting it right" and human flourishing can be assured by adhering to certain moral rules, codes, or standards. These may be self-imposed, imposed by society in general, or specified by some particular social or religious institution.

To be sure, rules and regulations are necessary for assuring a safe, orderly, and just society. But these cannot bestow life, and even perfect adherence to them does not constitute righteousness. The norm for "getting it right" in our lives remains God's own righteousness, as that is established by the gift of life itself.

Before leaving this passage, it is worth pondering the apostle's choice of Abraham as his example of faith. Why Abraham and not Jesus? And if Abraham, why not Sarah, too?

Models of Faith

As for Sarah, her secondary role in this passage reflects the subordinate role to which women were often consigned in antiquity. Although here Paul used Jewish traditions about Abraham's faith without modifying them to include a mention of Sarah's faith, elsewhere he names and honors various women of faith who were his associates in ministry and leaders in his congregations (for example, Romans 16:1-16). We should not allow this passage to mislead us into thinking that only men can be models for faith.

As for Jesus, Paul regarded him as much more than a mere role model. Jesus represents who God is for us, not the kind of person we are supposed to be for God. Faith does not call us to "be like Jesus," to strive for some impossible ideal. Faith means embracing our own humanity by trusting in the promise of God as that which has been disclosed, to the eyes of faith, in Christ's death and resurrection (3:24-25; 4:24-25).

Dimension 4:
A Daily Bible Journey Plan

Day 1: **Romans 1:1-17**

Day 2: **Romans 1:18–2:11**

Day 3: **Romans 2:12-29**

Day 4: **Romans 3:1-20**

Day 5: **Romans 3:21-31**

Day 6: **Romans 4:1-25**

Day 7: **Romans 5:1-21**

2

A Vision of Freedom

What to Watch For

The focus passage for this session is Romans 8:18-39. Paul wrote first about the hope that humanity shares with the whole of creation, which makes any present suffering seem slight by comparison. In this connection, he described how the Spirit helps us in our weakness, and expresses his confidence in the goodness of God's purpose. Most of all, he emphasized the confidence that comes from an experience of God's love, as that demonstrated in God's giving up of his only Son to death.

Among the key points in this passage:
➤ God's Spirit remains a vital presence with us during this time of hoping and waiting for redemption.
➤ Living in hope means living with the confidence that nothing lies beyond the scope of God's good purposes. In this present life we remain subject to all of the limitations imposed by our own humanity and to various threats that are beyond our control; but we can nevertheless live with the confidence that God is "for us," and that nothing can separate us from God's love.

11

1. Who are the two intercessors identified in this passage?

2. What, exactly, does creation long for?

3. What, exactly, does humanity long for?

4. What specific purposes (actions) are attributed to God in this passage?

Dimension 2:
What Does the Bible Mean?

The section of Romans from which our focus passage comes deals with a number of significant themes.

AN OUTLINE OF ROMANS 6-8	
The rule of God's grace	6:1–7:6
From death to life	6:1-14
From slavery to freedom	6:15–7:6
The role of God's law	7:7-25
The power of God's Spirit	8:1-17
God's gift of hope	8:18-30
God's love in Christ	8:31-39

The Paradox of Freedom

One significant theme in Romans is the theme of freedom, which, in Romans 6:15–7:6 has a double reference. On the one hand, Paul thought of freedom from sin (6:18, 20, 22), by which he meant slavery to one's own self-serving ambitions and finite visions of what really matters. At the same time, he thought about freedom for a new life, which he sometimes characterized with the one word *righteousness* (for example, in 6:13, 16, 20).

Paul was quite aware of the paradox that is involved here. True freedom depends not just on being *freed from* something, but also on being *freed for* (bound over to) a new commitment. He therefore described those who are in Christ as persons who have been "set free from sin" and, with that, "have become slaves of righteousness" (6:18). The new "slavery" is not like the old, however. Slavery to sin diminishes humanity, because it is a turning in upon oneself, and therefore a turning away from the source of all life. Slavery to righteousness, however, allows a flourishing of one's humanity, because it means opening one's life to the rule of God's grace (6:14). In summing up, Paul distinguished the two different kinds of slavery in yet another way: "we are slaves not under the old written code but in the new life of the Spirit" (7:6).

THE HOLY SPIRIT

What Paul said about the Holy Spirit in Romans is typical of what he said in his other letters. He did not think of the Spirit as simply an inner religious "feeling" or "attitude," but identified it above all with the power of God (Romans 8:13; 15:13, 19) that brings life (7:6; 8:2, 10-11; also 1:4). The contrast between "walking" (living) according to the Spirit and according to "the flesh" (8:4-6, 14) is a contrast between accepting one's life as a gift from God and presuming to be able to live out of one's own human resources. The Spirit is called "Holy" (5:5; 9:1; 14:17; 15:13, 16, 19; also 1:4) because its presence inscribes our lives as belonging to God.

For Paul, the Spirit is the harbinger of God's coming rule (14:17) and, as such, is the bearer of God's love (5:5; 15:30). Although he ordinarily associates the Spirit with God (as in 8:14; 15:19), in 8:9 he associates it both with God and with Christ. Neither in Romans nor elsewhere did Paul reflect on how, exactly, God, Christ, and the Spirit are related. It was a number of decades after the apostle's death before doctrines of the Trinity began to be formulated.

Joint Heirs With Christ

The concept of freedom also resurfaces, beginning with the declaration that "the law of the Spirit of life in Christ Jesus has set you free from the law of sin and of death" (8:2). The righteousness for which one is freed is now specifically linked with the enlivening presence of God's Spirit (8:10-11) and with our being "adopted" as God's children (8:12-16). As God's children, said Paul, we are also God's heirs. Indeed, we are "joint heirs with Christ," who is God's Son (8:17). It is specifically this last remark that prompts the comments about hope with which our focus passage opens (8:18-30).

The hope of which Paul wrote is the hope of sharing God's "glory." Here (8:18), as earlier in the letter (5:2-4), the coming glory is contrasted with the travail and suffering that is part of our present human condition. (See also 2 Corinthians 4:17.) God's glory, like the Holy Spirit, is associated by Paul with the power of the coming kingdom of God (1 Thessalonians 2:12). He believed that inheriting the Kingdom will mean the transformation of our present, vulnerable bodies (1 Corinthians 15:43; Philippians 3:21).

Meanwhile, however, we may live in hope, because God's Spirit has already been given us as the "first fruits" of what is to come (Romans 8:23-25).

FIRST FRUITS

In ancient Israel, the very first of a crop that could be harvested (the "first fruits") was ceremoniously consecrated to God, an acknowledgment that "the earth is the Lord's and all that is in it" (Psalm 24:1). In Romans 8:23 Paul referred metaphorically to the Spirit as "the first fruits," meaning the first part of the harvest of salvation ("glory").

The full harvest is yet to come, but that is assured by the reality of what is already present and being experienced through the Spirit. In Second Corinthians, making the same point with a business metaphor, he described the Spirit as a "downpayment" on what is still to be given (NRSV translates as "first installment" in 1:22 and as "guarantee" in 5:5).

All of Creation Longs for Deliverance

What is to come, according to Paul (8:23), is the fulfillment of our "adoption" as God's children and heirs (see 8:14-17), and with this, "the redemption of our bodies." To be "redeemed" means to be set free, and in this passage Paul is thinking specifically of our ultimate freedom from mortality—from the limitations, frailities, and travail that go along with being human. This idea is especially clear in 8:19-22, where the apostle articulates a vision of freedom that encompasses nothing less than the whole of God's creation. By definition, creation is finite, which makes it both subject to decay and vulnerable to sudden destruction. Paul believed that all of creation longs for deliverance from this bondage, and that this freedom is likewise the will of the Creator.

The fulfillment of this hope, for the natural world as well as for humankind, will be the unrestricted experience of God's "glory" (8:18, 20)—or, as Paul also put it, being "glorified" (8:30). He recognized that this will require the transformation of all things from a perishable to an imperishable mode of existence (see 1 Corinthians 15:42-44, 51-57). Yet the "glory" itself is not just being "imperishable." For Paul, being "glorified" meant entering fully into God's presence—into the "realm" (or "Kingdom") where God is "all in all" (1 Corinthians 15:28, 50).

However, Paul's real concern was not to speculate about what, exactly, creation's deliverance from decay will involve. Because the future belongs to God, so does the present, and it is the present life on which Paul was mainly focused, not only in this passage but elsewhere. He likened the "groaning" of creation to the pains of a woman in labor (Romans 8:22-23) because he believed that despite the trials and hardships of life, there is a larger meaning that God will reveal. He reminded his readers that true hope, by definition, remains "unseen" (8:24-25); to try to spell it out would only dissolve it into a list of trite human wishes. The present, said Paul, is a time for patient waiting (8:25) and for prayer in which we are assisted by the Spirit's continuing presence (8:26-27).

Paul Affirmed the Goodness of God $\mathcal{5}$

The remainder of this passage consists of two powerful expressions of faith. In the first (8:28-30), the apostle affirmed the goodness of God's purposes and, therefore, the ultimate meaningfulness of life. In this context, *foreknowledge* does not mean that God knows everything that is ever going to happen, but that the future has been claimed for God's good purposes. Similarly, to be "predestined" and "called" by God means to be "tagged" as God's people, brought into relationship to God ("justified") and, ultimately, into full communion with God ("glorified"). The past tense signals the certainty of this hope, not that it is

What then are we to say about these things? If God is for us, who is against us?
Roman 8:31

already fulfilled. There is nothing here about God's not calling certain people; doctrines of "double predestination" develop much later and can find no support in Paul's letters.

In Romans 8:29, the apostle said that God's people have been marked out to be "conformed to the image of" Christ, God's own Son (see also 1 Corinthians 15:49; 2 Corinthians 4:4). This is why believers have been described as God's "children," and therefore "joint heirs with Christ" of God's glory (8:15-17). It is also why Paul could begin a second affirmation of faith (8:31-39) with the simple but powerful assurance that "God is for us." The evidence for this is God's giving up "his own Son . . . for all of us" (8:32), which Paul interpreted as an act of unconditional, redemptive love (8:35, 37, 39; also 5:6-11; 2 Corinthians 5:14-21). Humanity's ultimate freedom—and glory—is to be found in the sovereign power of God's love, through which it is delivered both from bondage to its own mortality and from every conceivable threat, whether now or in the future (8:38-39).

Dimension 3:
What Does the Bible Mean to Us?

Christians Are Not Exempt From Suffering

The vision of freedom that finds expression in Romans 8:18-39 cannot be isolated from the understanding of hope that is present here; and Paul's conception of hope was inseparable from his belief in the God whose love has been disclosed in Jesus Christ. But as we reflect on how this passage can deepen and strengthen our own faith, it is important to recognize the astonishing breadth of Paul's vision. It encompasses not only the whole of humankind but the whole of creation. His vision of God's purposes and of God's love, and therefore of freedom and of hope, is correspondingly broad—far larger than our merely private visions of freedom or our individual experiences and hopes.

One of the striking features of this passage is the forthright way that Paul referred to the tribulations, risks, and threats that mark and mar our lives in this present age. He did not regard faith as an insulation from these trials, nor did he ever suggest that believers will suffer less than nonbelievers. In fact, the perils that he listed in verse 35 are exemplary of those that believers must face from society at large precisely because of their commitment to Christ.

Neither did Paul suggest that Christians are somehow exempt from what we would think of as the "ordinary" trials and tribulations of human existence. Some of these are listed in verses 38-39.

16

How, then, does the apostle respond to this situation? Two points are clear.

- Paul acknowledged that life in this world is perilous and that suffering is real. His comments remind us that the Christian response to suffering is not to deny that it exists, but to name it and to take it seriously. Christians take it seriously not only by offering consolation to those who suffer, and seeking to relieve their suffering. Taking it seriously also means attacking the causes and conditions that lead to suffering, insofar as those can be identified, anticipated, and eliminated.

> Believers must still face the reality of death, the assorted perils of daily life, the fear of what tomorrow might bring, and various terrors that lie quite beyond human control.

- Paul did not attribute human suffering to God, nor did he describe it as being God's will. He certainly did not commend suffering as something that believers should seek. When he said, just before our focus passage, that we will be "glorified" with Christ "if, in fact, we suffer with him" (Romans 8:17), the emphasis falls on the words *with him*. Suffering is not being encouraged as something good or as a condition for salvation. The point is, rather, that we are better able to cope with suffering when we face it with the confidence of those who have experienced the meaning of Christ's suffering. In his suffering and death faith perceives the all-embracing love of God, gracing us with new life and establishing us in a hope that enables us to look beyond the trials and tribulations of this present age.

In short, Paul did not deal with suffering by trying to deny its reality or to minimize its impact on our lives. He dealt with it by affirming the profound and decisive reality of God: that God's purposes are good (28-30) and that "God is for us" (31-39).

The Earth and Its Fullness Are the Lord's

Another remarkable feature of this passage is Paul's linking of humanity's destiny with the destiny of the natural world. The entirety of creation—both animate and inanimate, both human beings and their physical environment—is encompassed by the apostle's vision of God's liberating love.

In distinction from certain other religions in antiquity, and also from certain later, "off-center" forms of Christianity, Paul did not conceive of redemption as humanity's liberation from the created order. Here he was thinking of humanity's liberation along with the created order. He believed that "all things come from God" (1 Corinthians 11:12), so that "the earth and its fullness are the Lord's" (1 Corinthians 10:26, quoting Psalm 24:1). This is why he could say that hope is no less a reality for the nonhuman realm than for the human (Romans 8:20-21, 24).

The hope of which Paul wrote marks the present no less than the future as belonging to God. For humankind, the "waiting" to which he refers involves affirming the present as God's gift and taking responsibility for it.

Modern research has given us compelling scientific reasons to be concerned for our physical environment. The natural world and humankind are absolutely interdependent: the one is as fragile as the other, and each must depend on the other for its survival. Romans 8 presents us with an equally compelling theological reason to care for the world. Like our own life, the world of nature belongs to God and is an expression of God's love. Just as nature glorifies God through its produce and its beauty, so humanity's calling is to glorify God through its stewardship of all of life, including the place of its habitation.

Therefore, when Paul refers to both the natural world and humankind as "waiting" for the hope of redemption (19, 23, 25), he was not thinking of passive indifference to the present. Where hope is real the present has already been enlarged and enlivened. The sign that is found in many bus and train stations reminds of this: "Waiting Room, No Loitering." People who are truly "waiting" are alive to the present and affirm it as full of meaning; loiterers, we say, are "only killing time."

Dimension 4:
A Daily Bible Journey Plan

Day 1: **Romans 6:1-14**

Day 2: **Romans 6:15–7:6**

Day 3: **Romans 7:7-25**

Day 4: **Romans 8:1-11**

Day 5: **Romans 8:12-27**

Day 6: **Romans 8:28-39**

Day 7: **Romans 9:1-18**

CHRISTIANS AND JEWS

What to Watch For

Romans 11:11-36 must be read in connection with the whole of chapters 9–11. These chapters open with Paul expressing his deep concern for the situation of his "own people" (9:1-5), historic "Israel." His anguished question is why Israel in general has been unreceptive to the gospel of Christ. As you read, watch for the following emphases:

➤ In Romans 11:1-24, the apostle emphasized that God has remained faithful to Israel despite her unfaithfulness (11:1-10); that the Gentile world is included within God's plan of salvation (11:11-16); and that the reality of God's faithfulness in no way diminishes the need for faith on the part of both Jews and Gentiles (11:17-24). The last paragraphs (11:25-36) conclude the whole of chapters 9–11. (See the information in "An Outline of Romans 9–11" on page 22.)

➤ Rather than condemning unbelief or calling down God's wrath upon unbelievers, Paul affirmed the scope of God's faithfulness and the wideness of God's mercy.

➤ Paul concluded his discussion, not with a call to go evangelize the Jews, but with a hymn in praise of God's wondrous ways.

1. In the metaphor of 11:17-24, who are "the branches" and who are "the natural branches"? *Gentiles*

2. What is the "mystery" that Paul hopes his readers will be able to understand? *Israel was Saved.*

3. How does Paul characterize "the gifts and the calling of God"? *irrevocable*

4. According to this passage, what awaits those who are presently "disobedient"?

Getting in Touch With Paul

In order to appreciate what Paul was driving at in Romans 11:11-36, we must keep three important points in mind.

1. **Paul was a Jew.** Never, even as a Christian, did he reject or lose his Jewish identity. He not only acknowledged, but more than once emphasized his Jewishness. (See the box entitled, "Paul's Jewish Heritage").

    As a young man, Paul may have studied in Jerusalem with the noted teacher of the law, Gamaliel (Acts 22:3), although he himself never mentioned this. However, he did identify himself as having been associated with the Pharisees, a group that was dedicated to the interpretation of the law of Moses and its strict application to daily life (Philippians 3:5; also Galatians 1:14). This commitment to the law led Paul, during his years as a Pharisee, to become a determined persecutor of the church (1 Corinthians 15:9; Galatians 1:13, 23; Philippians 3:6.)

20

The apostle's knowledge of the Jewish Scriptures (the church's "Old Testament"), and the methods that he continued to use to interpret them, are further marks of the lasting importance of his Jewish upbringing. So is his comment about salvation coming first to the Jews (Romans 1:16; see also 2:10), and, especially, his long and earnest discussion, in Romans 9–11, of Israel's destiny.

PAUL'S JEWISH HERITAGE

Like most Jews in his day, Paul was not a native Palestinian but belonged to the Jewish Diaspora (Jews who were "scattered" throughout the Mediterranean world). According to Acts 22:3, he was a native of the city of Tarsus in Asia Minor (present-day Turkey). At that time, Tarsus was a major center of Hellenistic culture, and that, too, was an important part of his heritage. Yet even as a Christian, Paul continued to identify himself with the Jews. He described himself as "a member of the people of Israel, of the tribe of Benjamin, a Hebrew born of Hebrews" (Philippians 3:5), and further, as an "Israelite" descended from Abraham (2 Corinthians 11:22; also Romans 11:1). Like all Jewish males born to observant parents, he had been ceremoniously "circumcised on the eighth day" after his birth (Philippians 3:5).

(Adapted from *Harper's Bible Dictionary*, HarperSanFrancisco, 1985; page 331)

2. **What we often think of as Paul's "conversion" to Christianity he referred to as his "call" to apostleship.** Our word *conversion* suggests that one religion has been given up for another. This is not what Paul understood himself to have done. He did not think of Judaism and Christianity as two different religions. As he saw it, the gospel did not displace Judaism, but represented the truth that God had already disclosed to Israel and that Israel herself had not fully perceived. For this reason Paul regarded the true descendants of Abraham as those who believed in Christ, whether they be Jews or Gentiles (Galatians 3:6-9, 28-29).

3. The third point to bear in mind is that **our focus passage comprises the closing paragraphs of a discussion that Paul had launched at the beginning of chapter 9** (see "An Outline of Romans 9–11").

Gamaliel [guh-may'lee-uhl] was a Pharisee in the Sanhedrin. He may have been one of Paul's teachers (Acts 22:3). He counseled that the apostles be freed from their imprisonment (Acts 5:34-39).

AN OUTLINE OF ROMANS 9–11

Introduction: God's people, "Israel"	9:1-5
God's calling (election) of Israel	9:6-29
God's faithfulness toward Israel	9:30–10:21
Christ, the end of the law	9:30–10:4
Faith and unbelief	10:5-21
The scope of God's faithfulness	11:1-24
A remnant of Israel	11:1-10
Israel and the Gentiles	11:11-16
The importance of faith	11:17-24
Conclusion	11:25-36
The wideness of God's mercy	11:25-32
An ode to God's gracious wisdom	11:33-36

The Faithfulness of God

The question that occupied Paul throughout these chapters is why most Jews remained unbelievers, despite the fact that the gospel discloses the truth about Israel's God and God's promises to Israel (see, for example, Romans 9:1-5). Our excerpt from this long discussion enables us to see how Paul resolved the matter, and also provides us with some of the reasoning that lies behind his conclusion.

A fundamental and recurring theme in Romans is the unconditional and unrelenting faithfulness of God (for example, 3:3-4). This theme is especially important in chapters 9–11, where Paul emphasized that God remains faithful to Israel despite Israel's unfaithfulness to God (thus 10:21, quoting Isaiah 65:2). He did not mean that God had been faithful only to Israel. Another important theme in the letter is God's impartiality (2:9-11). This, too, is emphasized in chapters 9–11—quite succinctly in 10:11-13; more extensively in 11:1-24; and most eloquently in the paragraphs that conclude the whole discussion (11:25-36).

After acknowledging that at least some of Israel believed in the gospel (a "remnant," 11:1-10), Paul turned to the situation of the majority who had not (11:11-12). Would they remain forever alienated from God's promises? Definitely not, he said, because their unbelief had provided an opportunity for carrying the gospel to the Gentiles. The apostle saw this to be the outworking of God's purpose—although he did not say this explicitly until a bit later (11:32, 33).

God's plan had two phases:

1. The Jews had declined to believe in order to open the way for a mission to Gentiles (11:11).

2. The Gentiles had believed in order to make Israel "jealous," so that Israel, too, would come to believe (11:12, 13-14).

Do Not Be Proud; Stand in Awe

In this way, God's life-giving power embraces the whole of creation (11:15). This was the point of the metaphors in 11:16: the believing remnant in Israel was the assurance that the whole of Israel would be saved; and Israel's believing was the assurance that the whole world would be reconciled to God.

The metaphor of the olive tree (11:17-24) both summarizes the discussion thus far and served as a warning to Paul's Gentile Christian readers. Historic Israel is portrayed as a cultivated olive tree whose branches (unbelieving Jews) have been lopped off. This makes way for the branches of a wild olive tree (Gentiles) to be grafted on. Thus Gentiles have come to share in the riches of God's promises to historic Israel. But God's kindness is not to be taken for granted any more by the Gentiles than by the Jews. The life-giving and renewing grace of God is unconditionally given, but it must be received by faith—by trusting in God. This means surrendering all pretentious claims to having some privileged status with God. Paul's warning, "Do not become proud, but stand in awe" (11:20), is not a bad summary of what he means by faith: setting aside presumptuous claims about our own status, and receiving life as a wondrous gift from a faithful God.

The remainder of chapter 11 serves as a two-part conclusion to the whole of chapters 9–11. In the first part (11:25-32), the apostle recapitulated what he had just said about the inclusive scope of God's faithfulness. He called this a "mystery" because he took it to be an expression of the wisdom of God, which passes all human understanding. Israel's failure to believe and also the Gentiles' willingness to believe both had a purpose: Israel's unbelief was to allow the gospel to be preached to the Gentiles, and when "the full number of the Gentiles" had come to believe, then Israel, too, would be saved (11:25-27, with scriptural quotations from Isaiah 59:20 and 27:9).

God's Plan Is Wide and Deep

Paul wasn't thinking of what he or other apostles might be able to accomplish by stepping up their mission to the Gentiles, and then turning to an equally vigorous evangelization of the Jews. He was thinking in larger and more ultimate terms. His vision was of God's plan for salvation, and of fulfillment of God's purposes for humankind. Of one thing he was absolutely certain: "the gifts and the calling of God are irrevocable" (Romans 11:29; also 11:1); God remains faithful despite any appearances to the contrary. Whatever the measure of humanity's disobedience, God's mercy is wider and deeper—and completely decisive (11:32).

The second part of Paul's conclusion (11:33-36) is a carefully com-

23

posed hymn of praise to God's gracious wisdom. A threefold reference to God's "riches," "wisdom," and "knowledge" (33) is followed by three rhetorical questions (34-35, in part quoting from Isaiah 40:13), a threefold declaration of God's all-encompassing power (Romans 11:36a), and a short doxology (36b).

"The gifts and the calling of God are irrevocable" (Romans 11:29).

The three questions correspond (in reverse order) to the references in the opening line, and each presumes a negative response: no one can plumb the depths of God's knowledge; no one can provide any counsel that is equal to God's own wisdom; and no one can offer God any gift sufficient to merit the riches of God's unconditional grace. Because it is this grace that constitutes God's power, the declaration that all things belong to God does not lead to a cry of resignation, as one might expect. It leads, rather, to a joyful doxology.

Dimension 3:
What Does the Bible Mean to Us?

The Relationship of Christianity to Judaism

Our focus passage invites us to reflect on the relationship of Christianity to Judaism. The question is not only how these two historic religions are related. There are also more specific questions:

● What policies should our national and international church bodies adopt toward the Jews and Judaism?
● How should local churches relate to any Jews and Jewish congregations in their community?
● Should Christians try to convert the Jews?

Before we consider how Paul may inform our thinking about such questions, we must recognize that the context in which we are raising them is vastly different from the context in his day.

We live in a post-Holocaust age. The atrocities committed against the Jews during the 1930's and 1940's cannot and must not be forgotten. Behind those Nazi horrors stood long centuries of Christian anti-Semitism, and not only in Germany. In general, the church remained indifferent to the plight of the Jews under Hitler. The church continues to bear the shame and guilt of that indifference. Unquestionably, the Holocaust has forever changed the terms of Christian-Jewish dialogue.

In Paul's day there were two distinct forms of Christianity, Jewish and Gentile. Jewish Christianity was centered in Jerusalem under the leadership of Peter and James. Gentile Christianity was largely the result of

Paul's own missionary efforts—although even his predominantly Gentile congregations included some Jewish Christians.

In our day, however, the church is overwhelmingly "Gentile," and there is no distinctly Jewish form of Christianity. In fact, the poison of anti-Semitism continues to be present not only in our society, but often within our churches.

Paul's comments about the Jews were offered mainly in the context of his disputes with other Jewish Christians about the meaning of the gospel. It is important to remember that even Romans 9–11 was written for the Christians in Rome (who were mainly Gentiles), not for non-believing Jews.

Today, however, because there are so few Christians of Jewish descent, the primary question is not about the relation of Jewish and Gentile Christianity within the church. It is about Christianity's relationship to Judaism.

In Paul's day Judaism was still centered in the Jerusalem Temple, with its priesthood and sacrificial rites. Judea's Roman overlords regarded Christianity as a peculiar Jewish sect. And the Jews viewed Christians as a potential threat to their own precarious status as a tolerated religion.

In our day, Judaism exists without a temple, as it has since the first century. Modern Israel is a thoroughly secular state. And many Jews, both inside and outside of Israel, are either not "observant" of their religious traditions, or else decline even to regard themselves as Jewish in any religious sense.

Paul and the Christianity of his day believed that the world was almost at an end and that Christ would soon return to usher in God's reign (1 Corinthians 7:29-31; 15:24-28). The apostle was therefore intent only on his immediate mission to the Gentiles. He seems to believe that salvation for the Jews was amply provided for by God, and would be accomplished at the Lord's coming.

Most Christians today cannot share Paul's dramatic expectations about the future. It has been almost two thousand years since Paul wrote to the Romans, and the world goes on. Moreover, we are now residents of a "global village," in which both Christians and Jews are far outnumbered by adherents of other religions. If not directly, at least through the media, religious pluralism is a fact of life throughout our world. Thus today, Jewish-Christian dialogue can only take place as part of a broader inter-religious dialogue.

In Christ, the Covenental Community Is Enlarged
Despite these important differences between Paul's situation and ours, Romans 9–11 can still inform our thinking in several fundamental ways.

The apostle reminds us of how much we Christians have in common with the Jews (see 9:4-5). We share a belief in one God. We have common ancestors in the faith. Jewish Scripture constitutes our "Old Testament." Above all, as Paul specifically points out, Jesus of Nazareth, whom we affirm as "Messiah," was himself a Jew.

Paul also reminds us that Christianity and Judaism have experienced and appropriated this heritage in different ways. The church interprets God's self-disclosure, even in Israel's history, on the basis of its faith in Jesus as God's Son. Accordingly, not the law but Christ is affirmed as definitive of God's grace and claim (thus 9:30–10:4); and in Christ, the covenant community is enlarged to include the whole of humankind. Christians and Jews cannot affirm one another until they are honest about these differences and have come to appreciate what is distinctive about their experiences of God's grace.

Paul suggested that Jews who do not accept the gospel, no less than Gentiles who do, contribute to the outworking of God's purposes. Unbelieving Jews are still God's people (11:1-2). Paul remained confident about their salvation (11:26-32). He neither called down God's wrath on their unbelief nor presumed that the church must try to evangelize them. Their salvation is in God's hands, and it will be by God's grace.

Finally, Paul's metaphor of the olive tree continues to have a message for us. No one, including Christians, can claim any kind of privileged status with God. True faith (trusting in God's grace) means giving up all such claims. To trust in God is to affirm the wideness of God's mercy, and all of humankind, both "believers" and "unbelievers," are embraced by God's saving purpose.

The Temple site as it looks today.

Day 1: Romans 9:19–10:4

Day 2: Romans 10:5-21

Day 3: Romans 11:1-16

Day 4: Romans 11:17-36

Day 5: Romans 12:1-13

Day 6: Romans 12:14–13:7

Day 7: Romans 13:8-14

Romans 12:1-21

4

DISCOVERING WHAT IS GOOD

What to Watch For

The focus passage for this session is Romans 12:1-21, which opens the last major section of the letter. The initial and most fundamental appeal (12:1-2) is based on the affirmations that predominate in chapters 1–11, and is itself the basis of the exhortations that predominate in 12:3 through 15:13. This introductory appeal identifies who believers are called to be, how they should understand themselves in relation to society, and what they are called to do. The assorted counsels and exhortations that follow are intended as illustrations.

In addition to the opening, fundamental appeal, there are several points in this passage that merit special attention. Among these are the following:

➤ the reference to the varied "gifts" with which members of Christ's body are graced;

➤ the emphasis placed on love;

➤ the counsels concerning relationships to "outsiders," including those who are hostile to the community of faith.

Dimension 1:
What Does the Bible Say?

1. According to Paul, for what purpose have believers been "transformed"?

2. What examples are given of the differing "gifts" with which the members of Christ's body have been graced?

3. In what respect are believers encouraged to "outdo one another"?

4. What advice is given here about wisdom?

Dimension 2:
What Does the Bible Mean?

The first two verses of Romans 12 presuppose everything that Paul has been saying in chapters 1–11.

AN OUTLINE OF ROMANS 12–16	
Appeals to pursue what is good	12:1–15:13
Introductory appeal	12:1-2
Assorted appeals	12:3–13:7
The timeliness of love	13:8-14
An appeal on behalf of "the weak"	14:1–15:13
Letter closing	15:14–16:23
Special concerns and plans	15:14-33
Commendation of Phoebe	16:1-2
Greetings and warnings	16:3-23
A doxology	16:25-27

The Importance of a Single Word

This double function of Romans 12:1-2 is signaled by the word, *therefore* (1). Because we have been embraced by the transforming power of God's love in Christ, *therefore* we are called to offer our lives to God. **Paul was not telling his readers what they must do in order to be saved. Rather, he was addressing us as persons whose lives have already been made new, and who are thereby summoned to affirm and express this newness in the way we live.** These two opening verses are so fundamental that they merit close and careful attention. We may consider, in turn, the basis, the content, and the goal of the appeal.

The basis on which Paul was now appealing to his readers is "the mercies of God." He had written about God's mercies in earlier sections of this letter, especially in chapters 4 (with reference to the promise given to Abraham and Sarah); 5–8 (emphasizing that God's love is unconditional); and 9–11 (emphasizing the inclusiveness of God's love). Therefore, what we find now in the closing chapters of Romans is not a moral harangue—an urging of the readers simply to "try harder" and "do more" to be good. **Because Paul was basing his appeals on what God has done, as disclosed in Christ, they constitute not a harangue but an invitation: to receive the new life that has been granted already, and to allow this gift, God's grace, to find concrete expression in daily conduct.** This distinctly Christian basis of the appeals is clear from an earlier summons in this letter, to "present yourselves to God as those who have been brought from death to life" (Romans 6:13).

Present Your Bodies to God

This brings us to the content of Paul's appeal in 12:1-2. His call to "present your bodies to God" (12:1) simply rephrased the earlier appeal to "present yourselves to God" (6:13); in the apostle's vocabulary, the word *body* referred to the entire human self. In both cases he borrowed language that was commonly used with reference to the offering of sacrifices in a temple (in the Temple of the Jews in Jerusalem as well as in pagan temples.) There are two important differences, however: the "sacrifice" that Christians are to offer is of themselves; and for this reason, theirs is always "a living sacrifice." This striking metaphor (animals offered in sacrifice had always been slaughtered) emphasizes that God's claim is no less unconditional than God's grace. The life that God has given is to be put entirely at God's disposal.

The offering of one's entire self to God is also described as "spiritual worship." A more literal, and perhaps the better translation, is "reasonable worship" (as in the New Revised Standard Version footnote). Here we are in touch with the goal of Paul's appeal. Elsewhere he affirmed and sometimes provided advice concerning the church's "regular" worship—its assembling for prayers, hymns, the reading and interpreting of Scripture, prophesying, and sharing in the Lord's Supper (for example, 1 Corinthians 11:17-34 and 14:26-

33). But here he referred to the kind of worship that is fulfilled as Christians seek to live out their faith every day of the week and in everything that they do. This is their "reasonable worship" because it means thinking through and reasoning out the practical implications of the gospel, both for themselves as individuals and for the church as a whole.

This same goal is implied by the exhortation to allow the transforming presence of God's grace to renew one's "mind." Paul used the word *mind* to designate one's capacity for assessing what is appropriate and important. Therefore, being "transformed" involves the radical reorientation of one's life, away from unthinking conformity to the values, claims, and priorities of "this world," and toward "the will of God—what is good and acceptable and perfect." For the will of God, Paul looked not to the commandments of the law but to the new reality of life in Christ, because he believed that Christ, not the law, embodies God's will. (See "The Will of God".)

THE WILL OF GOD

Paul referred to the will of God in several different connections (although translators sometimes employ other terms for the words *will* and *wills*). In two places he attributed his apostleship to God's will (1 Corinthians 1:1; 2 Corinthians 1:1). Elsewhere he referred to God's will as directing even his apostolic itinerary (Romans 1:10; 15:32; 1 Corinthians 4:19). Most often, however, his references were more general: to the way God chooses to deal with humankind (Romans 9:18, 22; 1 Corinthians 12:18; 15:38), including God's saving purpose accomplished in Christ (Galatians 1:4) and to what God requires of humankind (Romans 2:18; 12:2; 2 Corinthians 8:5; 1 Thessalonians 4:3; 5:18).

While he was a Pharisee, and like the typical Jew he described in Romans 2:17-21, Paul would have supposed that God's will is fully revealed in the law, as it is contained in Scripture and as it had been interpreted by many generations of learned scribes. As a Christian, however, Paul believed that Christ, not the law, is definitive of God's will. He acknowledged that the law offers certain pointers to God's will, but only insofar as it is read with the eyes of faith—in Christ. In Christ, one perceives that the entire law is summed up in the love commandment (Romans 13:8-10; Galatians 5:13-14), which Paul could therefore describe as "the law of Christ" (Galatians 6:2). This law of love is as boundless as the gift of God's love from which it derives. Neither ten commandments nor ten thousand are sufficient to show what it requires. Love requires everything—one's whole self. Paul therefore identified love as the one "debt" that can never be paid in full (Romans 13:8).

The Renewing of Our Minds

The "renewing of [believers'] minds" is not so that we will be better able to remember all of the scriptural commandments. It is so that we can be more discerning of what love may variously require within the constantly changing circumstances of our lives.

Paul certainly did not mean that Christians are on their own when it comes to finding out and embracing the will of God. Because life in Christ is also and always life in Christian community, the quest to discern what love requires is a corporate venture, rooted in the community's shared experience of God's love in Christ and empowered by the Spirit's guiding presence. We must remember that Paul addressed his counsel in Romans to a congregation. Moreover, he wrote to a specific congregation. His aim was not to spell out the particulars of God's will for all times and places. From Romans 12:3 through 15:13, he offered only selected and rather general illustrations of what love requires. His aim was to encourage the Roman church to be a community of Christian dialogue, moral discernment, and faithful action, ever attentive to the particulars of their own situation.

The rest of chapter 12 provides a good sample of what Paul did in the closing sections of this letter. He began by calling on his readers to be mindful that they constitute "one body in Christ" (12:3-8). He had developed this metaphor more fully in 1 Corinthians 12. Yet even in this briefer version in Romans, it constitutes a powerful reminder that by belonging to Christ believers become "members of one another." In this same connec-

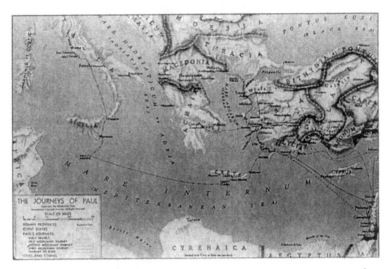

Corinth was established in the tenth century B.C. An important city, Paul was brought before the tribunal in Corinth (Acts 18:12-17).

tion, the apostle counseled his readers "to think with sober judgment" about themselves. For him, this was one important function of the "renewed mind," to enable believers honestly to assess their own strengths and weaknesses, to be self-critical. Paul's experience with his congregation in Corinth—the city from which he wrote—had already shown him how clambering for social and religious status can disrupt and divide Christian community, thereby violating the body of Christ.

The counsels in Romans 12:9 ("Let love be genuine; hate what is evil, hold fast to what is good") and 12:21 ("Do not be overcome by evil, but overcome evil with good") supply the framework for everything in between.

● Continuing his focus on the Christian community, Paul named various ways that genuine love should be manifested within the church (10-13). His examples include both attitudes, like "mutual affection" (10), and actions, such as assisting those in need (13).

● Then in verses 14-21, he urged that love should also be the mode of one's relationships with those who are outside the Christian community. His counsel of non-retaliation (19-20) is supported with quotations from Deuteronomy 32:35 and Proverbs 25:21-22.

● But his more radical appeal is that believers should bless those who persecute and curse them. In this case he may well be echoing a teaching that had been handed down from Jesus himself (see Matthew 5:44; Luke 6:27-28).

Dimension 3:
What Does the Bible Mean to Us?

A Series of Daring Counsels

Romans 12:1-21 prompts reflection on several very fundamental matters.
● What distinguishes the Christian ethic?
● What is involved in discerning the will of God?
● What does it mean for Christians, both as a community of faith and as individual believers, to continue living in the world without being of the world?
● And is our Christian responsibility to act in love even toward those who are hateful compatible with our responsibility to act justly and in support of a just society?

Let us consider, in turn, how Paul may help to inform our thinking on each of these points.

1. If we consult the moral teaching attributed to Jesus in the Gospels, we find little that was not present already in his own Jewish tradition—including the obligation to love God, to love the neighbor, to help the poor and needy, and to forgive. Indeed, the teachings conveyed in the Jesus tradition have been set within a distinctively Christian context. They have also been selected and arranged in ways that give them a special focus. Considered one by one, almost all of the moral precepts attributed to Jesus had been affirmed by others in his day, especially by other Jewish teachers but also by many in the pagan world.

What distinguishes the Christian ethic? Is there some uniquely "Christian" code of conduct?

The same holds true for the conduct that Paul commended in Romans 12:3-21. There was and is nothing uniquely Christian about humility, for example; or about being considerate of others, helpful, compassionate, hopeful, patient in suffering, and so on. Moreover, Jews, too, wanted to "serve the Lord" (in their case, meaning God), and Paul's counsel of nonretaliation was drawn in part from Jewish Scripture. What, then, is distinctive about the Christian ethic as the apostle conceived it?

Stated briefly, for Paul the distinctiveness of the Christian ethic is found not in what Christians are urged to do but in who they are called to be. As one New Testament scholar (Willi Marxsen) has put it, the Christian ethic is not about so-called "Christian actions," but about Christians acting. **This is why Paul's "therefore" in Romans 12:1 is so important: it reminds his readers that, by the grace of God they have "been brought from death to life."** It is this reality of grace, which believers experience as new life in Christ, that is to find expression in their conduct.

2. Paul did not resort to any pat answers, like "Do what Jesus would do," or "Do what I tell you," or "Do what Scripture teaches."

How can we know what grace requires, not just in general, but concretely? How can we know what God's will calls for in particular instances, when we have to make specific and difficult decisions?

Instead, he conceived the "discerning" of God's will to be a responsibility of the community of faith itself, and an ongoing task. Careful study, the weighing of all relevant facts, reasoned argument in the context of straightforward and respectful dialogue, earnest prayer, openness to the Spirit's leading, and admitting to the limits of human wisdom—all of this is involved in being a community of faith devoted to discerning and following the will of God.

For Paul, therefore, no rules, values, or virtues could ever have the status of "absolutes." That would be idolatry, because he believed that the one absolute reality is God's grace. Therefore, the actions that are most in accord with God's will are those that allow this grace—God's love as disclosed in Christ—to find expression in our lives and, through us, in the world. Although God's love

34

remains constant, as times and circumstances change, so may love's requirements. Therefore, the task of discerning God's will is never finished.

3. A third matter to which our passage calls attention is the ambiguous relationship that Christians have to "this age" (Romans 12:2, NRSV footnote). Paul was thinking of society, and of all the forces, known and unknown, with which we feel our present lives to be claimed,

> The question Paul challenges us to keep on asking is this: How in these particular circumstances, and given our present understanding of them, can we be agents of God's love?

and often threatened. On the one hand, "this age" is where we have been graced with the goodness of God's gift of life, and where we are called to be faithful stewards of God's love. On the other hand, our experience of grace also discloses that we do not really belong to this present age, but to the One by whose grace we live.

Therefore, not allowing ourselves to be "conformed to this world" does not mean trying to withdraw or insulate ourselves from society. Rather, it means not allowing our goals and priorities to be defined by the world's promises and claims. Moreover, believers are called to "be transformed" precisely in the world, not apart from it.

The apostle's own vision of how transformed people can contribute to a transformed society was very limited. This was partly because first-century Christians were a tiny, largely unrecognized minority in a society where only the privileged and well placed had access to power. In addition, Paul supposed that little time was left before this age would end, along with every social structure and institution. In spite of this, he knew that people who are truly transformed are also transformers, alive with the energy of God's love and committed to being its agents in the world.

Finally, what are we to make of the daring counsels to bless those who persecute us, repay no one evil for evil, and overcome evil with good (Romans 12:14-21)? Here Paul, like Jesus, stretches our concept of love's requirements almost to the breaking point. We are challenged to understand that authentic Christian love never asks the self-justifying question, "Who is my neighbor?" (Luke 10:29), which is actually the question, "Who deserves my love?" Authentic Christian love only asks *how* and *by what* specific actions one can be a neighbor (an agent of God's love) for this person or in this situation?

Love by no means requires us, nor does it even permit us, to be indifferent to evil. However, it does require that we respond to evil redemptively, not punitively, recognizing that the final judgment is God's alone (Romans 12:19). It requires us always to be self-critical, never presuming to wisdom that we do not have (Romans 12:16).

Day 1:	**Romans 14:1-12**
Day 2:	**Romans 14:13-23**
Day 3:	**Romans 15:1-13**
Day 4:	**Romans 15:14-33**
Day 5:	**Romans 16:1-16**
Day 6:	**Romans 16:17-27**
Day 7:	**1 Corinthians 1:1-17**

1 Corinthians 1:18–2:5

5

STRANGE WISDOM

What to Watch For

The focus passage for this session is 1 Corinthians 1:18–2:5, where Paul reflected on his "message about the cross" (1:18). He identified this message with the gospel through which the Corinthians were called to faith (2:1-5). Two pairs of contrasting terms are especially prominent in this discussion:

➤ wisdom and foolishness, and
➤ strength and weakness.

In each case, Paul contrasted what is true of God (or Christ) with what is true of this age (or the world):

➤ God's "foolishness," disclosed in the cross, is said to be wiser than the world's "wisdom"; and
➤ God's "weakness," also disclosed in the cross, is said to be more powerful than the world's "strength."

As Paul wrote this letter, his Corinthian congregation was at risk of tearing itself apart. Its members were competing with one another to secure the kind of status, power, and honor within the church that most of them did not have in society. Paul insisted that the gospel of "Jesus Christ and him crucified" turns all worldly values and priorities upside down, and that the Corinthian Christians themselves should realize that what had transformed them from "nobodies" to "somebodies" was their new life together in Christ (1:26-31).

1. According to Paul, what did "Jews" demand and what did "Greeks" desire?

2. By one count, Paul described Christ at least seven different ways in this passage. How many different ways can you find?

3. How did the apostle characterize his "preaching style" on the occasion of his first visit to Corinth?

4. What kind of "boasting" did Paul regard as appropriate? as inappropriate?

Dimension 2:
What Does the Bible Mean?

1 CORINTHIANS

Paul first visited Corinth in the year A.D. 50-51. Subsequently, he wrote several letters to the church that he had founded there. The earliest surviving letter is First Corinthians. This is not actually Paul's "first" letter to the church, however. In 1 Corinthians 5:9-11 he himself refers to a previous, misunderstood letter. When he wrote the letter that we know as "First Corinthians," Paul was in residence in the city of Ephesus, where he planned to remain until the following spring (16:8-9). After Pentecost he would return to Corinth by way of Macedonia (16:5-7), doubtless visiting his churches in places like Philippi and Thessalonica. Although a co-worker had already set out for Corinth by the same route, the apostle expected this letter to get there first (16:10).

Paul wrote First Corinthians for two principal reasons. First, he needed to answer a letter from the Corinthians (1 Corinthians 7:1). In that letter, which does not survive, the leaders of the church seem to have asked for his counsel on various specific matters, including sexual relationships, marriage, and divorce. Second, the apostle felt that he must respond to some unsettling news that he had heard about the Corinthian congregation, including the flourishing of rivalries (1:11); a case of sexual immorality (5:1); and indifference to those in need (11:18). Before concluding, he asked his readers to welcome Timothy (16:10-11); explained that Apollos (the favorite of some) would not be coming for a while (16:11); and summarized his own travel plans (16:3-9).

Paul Confronts the Church

Paul opened First Corinthians as he did most of his letters: the required address and salutation (1:1-3) are followed by a paragraph of thanksgiving (1:4-9). Then, without further introduction, he got right down to business. He had heard that rivalries and quarrels had erupted in his congregation, and he was worried that these might dilute and diminish its Christian witness, or even tear the church apart (1:10-13). It was particularly disturbing that competing factions were invoking his and Apollos' names to support their claims. The point of 1 Corinthians 1–4 was to try to put a stop to this practice. To do so, Paul emphasized that he and Apollos were only God's servants and ultimately accountable to God, just as was everyone else (3:5–4:5). He also parodied the proud boasts of the Corinthians about their spirituality, and contrasted their supposed religious status with his own miserable situation— dishonored, impoverished, his very life constantly at risk (4:6-13).

The discussion that begins in 1:18 and extends through chapter 2 may appear, at first, to be out of place within chapters 1–4.

The Strange "Wisdom" of the Cross

The troubles in the Corinthian church were temporarily out of view as Paul focused his readers' attention on the strange "wisdom" of the cross. However, his comments about the meaning of the cross form the theological basis on which he offered his critique of what was going on in the congregation. First, and most directly, these paragraphs support the appeals in chapters 1–4. Less directly, but no less surely, they also support all the rest of the appeals in this letter.

The apostle's discussion of wisdom may be divided into four main parts.

• In 1 Corinthians 1:18-25 Paul set forth the major points that he wanted his congregation to grasp.

39

- Next, in 1:26–2:5, he demonstrated the truth of these points by referring to evidence of which his readers had direct knowledge.
- In the third section, 2:6-13, Paul extended his discussion of God's wisdom with some comments about its "hiddenness," and the Spirit's role in disclosing what can be known of it.
- In conclusion, 2:14-16, noting how foolish God's wisdom seems to those who are not open to the Spirit's presence, he emphasized that the community of faith is informed and guided by "the mind of Christ." As elsewhere in his discussion, Paul was referring to the One whom he proclaimed as "Jesus Christ, and him crucified."

Our passage for this session comprises only the first two parts of the section, 1:18-25 and 1:26–2:5.

WISDOM IN CORINTH

Teachings about wisdom had a long and honored place within the Judaism of Paul's day. The wisdom valued by Jews was of the "practical" and "religious" sort. It was wisdom that could be set out in memorable pieces of advice like those in the Book of Proverbs. The Jewish Bible that became the church's earliest Scripture contained other Wisdom Literature as well, including the writings we know as the Wisdom of Solomon and the Wisdom of Jesus, Son of Sirach. (Most Protestants regard both of these as books of the "Old Testament Apocrypha.")

Even Paul's Gentile converts in Corinth were introduced to this Jewish wisdom tradition, perhaps by gifted teachers like Apollos as well as by the apostle himself. In addition, however, many of the Corinthian Christians were also influenced by prevailing Greek and Roman views about wisdom. According to these, true wisdom manifested itself in artful and persuasive oratory—in the high-flown speech of those who had been specifically trained and were especially skilled in the art of rhetoric. In a city like Corinth, rhetorical skill was an important means of advancing one's status. With status came honor. With honor came "connections." And with connections came power.

From "Nobodies" to "Somebodies"

In the Corinthian church, apparently, a concern for wisdom in the more specifically "religious" sense had been merged with the "secular" valuing of status, honor, and power. A spiritual elite seems to have developed—Christians who regarded themselves as privileged with special religious wisdom and skill in religious speech. Flaunting their "connections" with people like Paul, Cephas, and Apollos, they claimed to be of higher spiritual status, deserving of honor, and entitled to power. The rivalries that Paul lamented in 1 Corinthians 1:10-13 are symptoms of this situation.

In 1 Corinthians 1:18-25, Paul challenged the Corinthians' secularized religiosity by contrasting it with the gospel.

• He identified the gospel as his "message about the cross" (1:18), his preaching of "Christ crucified" (1:23).

• He declared that this gospel is the means through which God's saving power is present for those who are open to receive it (see especially, 1:18, 21).

• He emphasized that the wisdom and power of God are radically different from the wisdom and power that the world so eagerly seeks and highly rewards (1:19, 22-25). The world associates wisdom and power with wealth, status, honor, and control over others. The gospel, however, associates wisdom and power with the self-giving, others-affirming love of God disclosed in the cross and active in the believing community.

Elsewhere in his letters Paul quoted creedlike statements about Jesus' death as "sacrificial" or "substitutionary." Such statements had been in use in the church for some time before Paul's own call to the gospel. However, the apostle hadn't employed any of these traditional creedal statements in 1 Corinthians 1:18-2:5. In this passage we are closer to his own interpretation of Jesus' death. Paul viewed the cross as definitive of God's love, and as demonstrating that God is "for us" absolutely and unconditionally (see 2 Corinthians 5:14; Romans 5:6, 8; 8:31-39). The "wisdom" of the cross is that the saving power of God is the power of love. Over against the "conventional wisdom" of his day, Paul's gospel declares that life is a gift of God's love, and that it flourishes where God's people become agents of that love in and for the world. To support his claims about the gospel, the apostle appealed to his readers' own experience.

He reminded them that most in their congregation were not privileged with what, "by human standards," appears to be wisdom, status, honor, or power (1:26-31). In Corinthian society, with just a few exceptions, they remained "nobodies." Yet in Christ, and with no exceptions, they were "somebodies." Here Paul chose his words carefully, however: Christ Jesus "became for us" wisdom, righteousness, sanctification, and redemption (1:30). These were not "possessions" that the Corinthians could boast of as

41

religious status symbols (1:29). Their boast was to be only in the Lord (1:31, echoing Jeremiah 9:23-24), who is the crucified Christ. It is in him that they had been granted life and a status that the world can neither give nor take away.

The Corinthians would also remember what they experienced when Paul first came to their city preaching the gospel (1 Corinthians 2:1-5). He had not put his own rhetorical skill or "religious experience" on display. He had not exhibited any "personal charisma." He had not preached the popular, "conventional wisdom" about life. He had proclaimed only "Jesus Christ, and him crucified." Through this message about the cross, the Corinthians had experienced God's own saving power and had been graced with new life. Just as the cross is definitive of God's love and of their coming to faith, so must it be definitive for their lives in Christian community and their witness in the world. This message is what Paul wanted his congregation to understand.

Dimension 3:
What Does the Bible Mean to Us?

The "Wisdom" of the World

The contrast that Paul has drawn in this passage between the "wisdom" of the world and the "foolishness" of preaching "Jesus Christ, and him crucified" is often misinterpreted and misapplied.

To avoid misunderstanding, we must remember what kind of "wisdom" Paul had in mind as he wrote to the Corinthians. He was thinking, in part, of the self-referential displays of shallow knowledge that characterized the many secular orators and popular street-corner philosophers of the day. He was also, and perhaps more especially, thinking of many in the Corinthian church itself who claimed to have some kind of special religious wisdom that was not available to all believers.

Thus, the apostle was not being critical of knowledge as such. He was not disparaging humanity's God-given thirst to learn as much as possible about itself and its world. Our focus passage is not a put-down of those who are committed to continuing intellectual inquiry, reasoning things out, and deepening their understanding of what is already known.

The "Foolishness" of the Cross

It is equally important to recognize why Paul referred to the message of the cross as "foolishness." He meant that the cross seems like foolishness to anyone who measures wisdom by merely human standards. He did not mean that the gospel itself is unreasonable or unintelligible. Clearly, the apostle was spending his time and effort in this very passage to reason with the

Corinthians about the gospel and to help them understand it. He certainly did not mean that faith can dispense with learning or that knowledge has no bearing on faith. He was quite aware that faith is always seeking understanding, and that understanding can enrich faith and deepen it.

What, then, is the meaning of this passage for Christians today? For twentieth-century Christians, as for the Christians of first-century Corinth, it is a call to reconsider what constitutes true wisdom and power. Expressed more concretely, it challenges us to re-evaluate our notions about "the good life" and "success." In doing so, it pushes us to take stock of the priorities and commitments that define our hopes for the future and that shape our lives in the present.

Success . . . as Measured by the Cross

How might our lives be different if we were to take seriously Paul's message about the wisdom and power of the cross? What would happen if we replaced our striving for worldly status and honor with a celebration of the status that is given with life in Christ, the crucified Messiah? Specific answers to these questions are possible only where Christian people, both individually and in dialogue with others, take careful account of their own particular circumstances. Nevertheless, some general points are broadly applicable.

To begin with, because Paul's message about the cross challenges all "worldly" understandings of status, honor, and power, it also has important implications for how we relate to other people. Undoubtedly, the way we relate to others is shaped in large part by how we regard ourselves. Do we value ourselves as human beings? If so, on what basis? What are our priorities? How do we set them? By what measure do we judge ourselves to be "successful" or "fulfilled" as human beings and in our relationships with others? Although these questions are not specifically addressed in 1 Corinthians 1:18–2:5, we are left in no doubt about how Paul would answer them.

Paul's gospel calls us to accept ourselves as children of the God who is disclosed in Christ Jesus (see 1:30). This means that the "value" of our lives is never increased by anything that we can attain or acquire, and never decreased by anything that is done to us or taken from us. Our lives are valuable because they were given by God, the Giver from whom our breath is borrowed, and who remains the source and norm of everything valuable.

Because life is a gift of the Giver, our very highest calling as human

This passage does not spell out or seek to impose any particular theory about Christ's death. It does not try to explain exactly why Jesus had to die on a cross, or exactly how the cross "saves." For Paul himself, it was enough to speak of Christ's death as demonstrating God's unconditional love. He therefore proclaimed the cross as the means through which God's saving power becomes a life-changing presence for those who are open to receive it.

43

What "fulfills" our lives, according to Paul's gospel? By what measure can the truly "successful life" be identified? The answer that is given in 1 Corinthians 1:18–2:5 is clear: "Success" is to be measured by the cross!

beings is to glorify God (note 1:31, to "boast in the Lord"). Stewardship means respecting and honoring God's gift as it is manifested not only in one's own life but also in the lives of all other human beings and in the whole of creation.

To appreciate the radical character of Paul's claim, we must remember what crosses represented in his day. They were instruments of death, not life. They brought shame, not honor. They stripped all status and power away. They represented the opposite of everything that the world—"conventional wisdom"—valued most highly.

This, of course, is the apostle's point. His message about the cross sets God's wisdom over against the world's. Conventional wisdom thinks of success as "getting ahead," and regards wealth, social standing, and power as its fruits. When guided by this wisdom, we are encouraged to view other people, even those closest to us, as either helping us be "successful" or keeping us from being "successful."

According to the wisdom of the cross, however, "success" means embracing the status that is already ours by reason of God's gift of life. The fruit of this "success" is not "getting ahead" of others, but affirming them in love and joining with them to expand love's scope in our common life.

Dimension 4:
A Daily Bible Journey Plan

> *Day 1:* 1 Corinthians 1:18–2:5
>
> *Day 2:* 1 Corinthians 2:6-16
>
> *Day 3:* 1 Corinthians 3:1-23
>
> *Day 4:* 1 Corinthians 4:1-21
>
> *Day 5:* 1 Corinthians 5:1-13
>
> *Day 6:* 1 Corinthians 6:1-20
>
> *Day 7:* 1 Corinthians 7:1-24

1 Corinthians 7:1-24

6

PARTICULAR GIFTS

What to Watch For

The focus passage for this session is 1 Corinthians 7:1-24, part of a section of the letter in which Paul offered various counsels about sex, marriage, divorce, and being single. This agenda was not entirely his own, however. For the most part, he was responding to rather specific questions that he knew were being debated in his Corinthian congregation. These included, in turn:

➤ whether sexual activity was appropriate for Christians and, if so, under what conditions (1-6);
➤ whether marriage was appropriate for Christian singles and, if so, under what conditions (7, 8-9); and
➤ whether divorce and remarriage were permissible under any conditions (10-16).

Along with his specific counsels on these matters, and in support of them, the apostle offered general comments about the life to which Christians are "called" in the world (17-24). Paul insisted that the important point was not one's worldly status or circumstances. What really matters, he said, is whether, whatever the particular situation, one lives as in the presence of God.

45

1. In Paul's view, under certain conditions Christian spouses may abstain from sexual relations. What conditions did he mention?

2. Concerning what specific question did the apostle refer to a commandment of the Lord?

3. Did Paul believe that a marriage can work if one spouse is a Christian and the other is not?

4. According to Paul, what is more important than whether one has been circumcised (as a Jewish or Gentile Christian)?

Paul's Views Were Frequently Misunderstood

Paul's views concerning women, marriage, and sex are often misunderstood. A careful reading of 1 Corinthians 7 will help us see what the apostle actually thought, even if, at the end, he still does not seem to be saying what modern Christians might wish him to say. In order to let him speak on his own terms, we need to be alert to four special points.

1. Paul responded to specific questions that the Corinthian Christians raised with him in a letter (1a; see "An Outline of 1 Corinthians 5–7"). This means, for example, that we must not read 1 Corinthians 7 as if it represents Paul's carefully considered view of "Christian marriage" or "the Christian home." *Rather, he was dealing with issues that had come up in* **one** *particular congregation.* He was addressing the Corinthians' agenda, not his own.

AN OUTLINE OF 1 CORINTHIANS 5–7

Directions about an incestuous man	5:1-13
Counsels about going to pagan courts	6:1-11
Warnings about going to prostitutes	6:12-20
Responses to questions from Corinth	7:1-40
Introduction	7:1
About marriage	7:2-7
About widowers and widows	7:8-9
About divorce	7:10-16
Comments about life in society	7:17-24
About the unmarried	7:25-35
About the betrothed	7:36-38
Final comments	7:39-40

2. The fundamental dispute in Paul's congregation seems to have been about physical sexual intimacy. Is sex compatible with being a Christian, even when sex takes place in a Christian marriage? Apparently some in the Corinthian church thought not. For this reason they opposed marriage and urged those already married either to divorce or to abstain from sexual relations. Perhaps they could see no distinction between sex within marriage and sex outside marriage. Perhaps they were generalizing from Paul's own point that becoming "one flesh" with a prostitute violated a believer's relationship with the Lord (1 Corinthians 6:15-18).

This "anti-sex" sentiment is summarized in 1 Corinthians 7:1b, which the NRSV translators present as a quotation: Christians should not "have sex" under any circumstances. *From what Paul later said, this was clearly not his own view.* He never referred either to sex or to marriage as, by itself, evil.

3. Although Paul was single and wished that others could be, he recognized that his contentment with celibacy was a special "gift" not shared by all (7). Therefore, even though he commended the single state, he did not command it. However, even in commending singleness, Paul was departing from the cultural norms of his day. Most people thought of marriage as a duty, because they regarded its chief purpose as producing children.

Paul preferred being single because he believed that little time was left before Christ's return and the end of this world. All worldly institutions were in the process of passing away (29-32). For him, therefore, marriage had—quite literally—no future. In addition, he believed that one's commitments to a spouse inevitably compromised one's devotion to the Lord (32-35). He wanted to avoid this, because he believed that there was not much time left to spread the gospel. Although he knew that most other apostles were married (1 Corinthians 9:5), he seemed to fear that having a wife would slow him down too much.

4. Despite his concern to help the Corinthian Christians deal with their moral uncertainties, Paul declined to lay down any hard and fast rules about sex and marriage. He recognized that individual situations vary, and that what is appropriate in one instance may not be in another.

Paul's Reasons Were Theological and Practical

There are some points, however, on which Paul did not budge. For instance, he believed that sexual intimacy is only appropriate between partners who are mutually committed to their relationship and faithful to one another (2). He insisted that within a monogamous relationship intimacy is a mutual privilege and responsibility (3-4). Therefore, any decision to abstain from marital sex must be temporary, agreed to by both parties, and for the specific purpose of prayer (5-6). He called this allowance for temporary abstention from sex within a marriage a "concession," because he did not want his views to be confused with those of the "anti-sex" Christians in Corinth.

> Paul believed that sexual intimacy is only appropriate between partners who are mutually committed to their relationship and faithful to one another.

The apostle recognized that particular circumstances must be considered. In verses 8-9 he offered counsel to those who are single because a spouse has died. His general advice—not to marry again—was consistent with his own preference for being single. He said, however, that for those who lack this gift, it is better to marry again than to be led into promiscuity by strong sexual desires. This statement doesn't mean that Paul considered marriage only in terms of sex. He focused on its sexual aspect because that is what the Corinthians had asked him about.

Paul believed that sexual intimacy is only appropriate between partners who are mutually committed to their relationship and faithful to one another.

In verses 10-16 the apostle responded to questions about divorce. For the "anti-sex" Corinthians, divorce may have seemed like a better option than trying to maintain a "celibate marriage." However, the apostle disagreed (10-11), citing Jesus himself as his authority (see "Jesus and Divorce").

48

JESUS AND DIVORCE

Each of the Synoptic Gospels contains a saying about divorce that is attributed to Jesus (Matthew 5:32, 19:9; Mark 10:11-12; Luke 16:18), although no two versions are exactly alike. According to most scholars, the earliest form is the one in Mark, which in content seems to agree with the saying of Jesus to which Paul refers in 1 Corinthians 7:10-11.

We do not know exactly how Paul learned of Jesus' teaching about divorce. It could not have been from the Gospels, because even Mark, which is probably the earliest, dates from after the apostle's death. However, some collection of Jesus' sayings, in either oral or written form, must have been circulating from a fairly early time. It is likely that both Paul and the Gospel writers were acquainted with such a collection.

According to Mark, Jesus' comments on divorce were prompted by an encounter with some Pharisees (Mark 10:2-4).

When they asked him whether Moses' law permits divorce, Jesus turned the question back on them. They answered, correctly, that the law does allow a husband to divorce his wife (Deuteronomy 24:1-4; there is no provision for a wife to divorce her husband). Jesus, however, described this law as only a concession (Mark 10:5), and set his own view over against it: those whom "God has joined together" must remain together (Mark 10:6-9).

As Mark has it, Jesus' disciples later asked him to explain this. The rule that he formulated for them takes account of Roman law, which allowed a wife as well as a husband to initiate divorce. In either case, Jesus said, divorce followed by remarriage to another person constitutes adultery (Mark 10:10-12).

Matthew's version of this rule allows for one partial exception: a husband is permitted to divorce his wife if she has been guilty of some sexual immorality.

Live As One Claimed by God

(In the apostle's formulation of this rule, the verbs *separate* and *divorce* are used synonymously.) The parenthetical remark in verse 11 shows that Paul realized Christians may divorce anyway. His response, however, was not to condemn the persons involved, but to echo the second part of the Lord's commandment: after a divorce there must be no remarriage, except to the original spouse.

The apostle opposed divorce even where a Christian is married to a non-Christian (12-16). He reasoned that, if one partner is a believer, the children can be called "holy"; and if the children are holy, the unbelieving partner must be, too. However, if the unbelieving spouse wants a divorce,

49

it should be granted—despite the Lord's commandment. At least in the circumstance of these "mixed" marriages, Paul regarded God's call to "peace" as more binding than Jesus' rule against divorce.

Whatever a person's domestic situation or social circumstances, the most important thing is to live as one whose life is both given and claimed by God. No matter what a person's particular circumstances or gifts, it is one's relation to God that should shape one's conduct.

Dimension 3:
What Does the Bible Mean to Us?

Called to "Remain With God"

At first glance it would appear that the focus passage for this session offers straightforward answers to several of our important questions about the Christian life.

● How are Christians supposed to view sex?

● Is sexual pleasure to be affirmed, condemned, encouraged, or discouraged?

● Does Christianity regard some sexual activities and relationships as sinful?

● What should a Christian marriage be like?

● What does it mean to be a Christian husband, wife, parent, or child?

● Is divorce ever an acceptable option for Christians?

When we look at this passage more closely, however, we run into some complications. We discover, for example, that Paul was writing to a specific congregation about issues that had arisen in one particular context. We see that his views were influenced in part by an expectation about Christ's return that was not fulfilled. We are struck by the vast social and cultural distance that separates our world from Paul's. And we are reminded that the questions facing Christians today are in many respects different from those that confronted Christians two thousand years ago.

How can we bridge this distance in time and circumstance that separates us and our churches from Paul and his church in Corinth? We can take our cues from the apostle himself. All of the specific counsels in 1 Corinthians 7 are anchored in one fundamental conviction about the new life in Christ.

Paul believed that belonging to Christ profoundly alters the way we deal with the conditions and circumstances that the world imposes on us (17-24). He believed that Christ offers us an identity that diminishes the signficance of our gender, race, ethnic origin, economic class, social status, and the like. In Christ, these no longer define us, but only the place and conditions under which we are called to "remain with God."

The apostle conceived this remaining with God as a dynamic relationship, not as a static condition.

50

For him, it meant to "lead the life" (17, NRSV) that comes with belonging to Christ. This, his most fundamental point in 1 Corinthians 7, is no less true for us than it was for the Christians of first-century Corinth.

The apostle's own procedure with the Corinthians suggests how we must deal with his specific directives today. On each question that he took up, he was concerned to allow for differences in individual situations. He thought that marriage was best for some, but that being single was best for others. Given certain conditions he would favor remarriage, otherwise not. Overall he was against divorce, but in some cases he would commend it as the better course. Paul did not give up his basic conviction that we are called to "remain with God," whatever our specific circumstances. But he also recognized that circumstances vary from person to person, place to place, and time to time. He sought to take this into account as he formulated his counsels. We must take it into account, too, as we consider the meaning of Paul's counsels for today.

Sexual Promiscuity

Sexual promiscuity is one activity that Paul ruled out completely (2). His reason, "because of immorality," likely reflects the belief that sexual gratification apart from a committed relationship is self-indulgent and therefore self-destructive. We should have no problem affirming this, both on theological grounds provided by Paul's own gospel and because of what we learn from modern psychological, sociological, and medical research. We know more exactly than Paul could have known just how destructive sexual promiscuity can be, both of individuals and of the intricate fabric of personal and social relationships.

Another point that transcends the particular issues in Corinth is Paul's insistence that marriage must be a partnership of equals (3-6). His comment that each partner properly has "rights to" ("authority over," NRSV) the other may not express this very well. Nevertheless, his call for complete mutuality in marriage distinguishes him from most of his contemporaries. The apostle understood that belonging to Christ gives a new depth and meaning to every other relationship, including marriage. In their belonging to Christ a husband and wife are equals. Because each belongs to Christ, neither "belongs" to the other as if the other were superior.

Affection for One's Spouse

It is understandable that Paul said nothing about affection for one's spouse. This relatively modern concept is specific to certain cultures. However, his insistence on mutuality was a call for something more enduring—for each partner to respect, affirm, and care for the other. Today, as always, these are the foundation stones of every genuinely fulfilling relationship.

51

The apostle's preference for remaining single (7, 8-9) was very closely tied to his and the church's belief that little time was left before Christ's return. Very soon, however, the church had to begin rethinking this belief, and considering how to be Christian in a world that is both enduring and growing more complex. Without question, modern society presents radically new kinds of risks and opportunities, both for married and unmarried Christians. Divorce, too, is a more complex matter in our day than in Paul's (10-16). Perhaps better than he, we know the importance of stable and enduring marriages. We also know that the marital concord for which he was specifically concerned (15) is increasingly difficult to nourish and sustain in our modern world.

Finally, then, Paul's counsels about sex and marriage require us, as they required the Corinthians, to take careful account of the particular circumstances and situations within which we are called to "remain with God." In certain respects, they provide guidance that transcends the differences between our day and Paul's; but they were never intended to be taken as inflexible rules.

Dimension 4:
A Daily Bible Journey Plan

> *Day 1:* 1 Corinthians 7:25-40
>
> *Day 2:* 1 Corinthians 8:1-13
>
> *Day 3:* 1 Corinthians 9:1-27
>
> *Day 4:* 1 Corinthians 10:1-13
>
> *Day 5:* 1 Corinthians 10:14–11:1
>
> *Day 6:* 1 Corinthians 11:3-16
>
> *Day 7:* 1 Corinthians 11:17-34

1 Corinthians
8:1-13

7

NECESSARY KNOWLEDGE

What to Watch For

The focus passage for this session is 1 Corinthians 8:1-13, where Paul introduced the topic of "food sacrificed to idols" (8:1).

His Corinthian congregation was divided over the matter of eating meat that was known to have been ritually slaughtered in some pagan temple. Certain members of the congregation seemed to believe that such meat should remain out of bounds for Christians. Others argued that Christians were perfectly free to partake of it, because they knew that the gods to whom it was offered didn't really exist.

Paul laid the foundation for his response in 8:1-6, where he took account of what some Corinthians were claiming about their knowledge of God. For the apostle, however, the issue was less about "knowledge" than "love." He stated this idea generally in 8:1-3, as he opened his discussion, and then more concretely in 8:7-13, where he offered some specific counsels.

Other points in this passage that deserve special notice include:

➤ a two-part affirmation of faith (8:6);
➤ several occurrences of the word *conscience* (8:7, 10, 12); and
➤ Paul's references to Christ's death (8:11) and sinning against Christ (8:12).

1. Why is it appropriate to describe the statement in 8:6 as a two-part affirmation of faith?

2. According to Paul, what knowledge is it that "not everyone" has?

3. Paul referred to some of the Corinthians as "weak." What was their weakness, as he saw it?

4. How could one's dining in a pagan temple become a "stumbling block" to some fellow Christian?

Dimension 2:
What Does the Bible Mean?

AN OUTLINE OF 1 CORINTHIANS 8:1–11:1

Introduction	8:1-6
Knowledge and love	8:1-3
The One God	8:4-6
Counsels about "the weak"	8:7-13
The counsels supported	9:1-27
Introduction	9:1-3
Paul's right to material support	9:4-14
Paul's right to decline material support	9:15-18
Paul's missionary strategy	9:19-23
Conclusion	9:24-27
Warning about idolatry	10:1-22
The example of Israel	10:1-13
Pagan sacrifices	10:14-22
Further counsels about "the weak"	10:23-30
Summary appeal	10:31–11:1

What About Food Sacrificed to Idols?

In 1 Corinthians 8:1-6 Paul introduced the topic of "food sacrificed to idols." Perhaps the letter from Corinth (see 7:1) had asked for instructions about this, as well as for advice about sex and marriage. In any case, Paul's discussion of the topic extends through 11:1, with his most specific counsels appearing in 8:7-13 and 10:23-30 (see "An Outline of 1 Corinthians 8:1–11:1").

What About Pagan Sacrifices?

The issue that Paul addressed was whether Christians were allowed to eat meat that they knew or suspected to be left over from pagan rites (see "Pagan Sacrifices").

PAGAN SACRIFICES

In First Corinthians, Paul referred several times to food that was "sacrificed [sometimes translated 'offered'] to idols" (8:1, 4, 7, 10; 10:19). This expression was coined by the Jews, then used also by the Christians, to describe the animal sacrifices that were ritually offered in pagan temples. The Jews themselves continued to offer similar sacrifices in their Temple in Jerusalem. These ceased only with the destruction of the Jewish Temple by the Romans in A.D. 70.

Customarily, only part of the sacrificial animal was offered up to the pagan deity, usually by burning on the altar. The remainder was kept back as the god's gift to his or her worshipers. Sometimes this leftover meat was eaten in the temple precinct (1 Corinthians 8:10), sometimes it was taken home to eat (10:27-29), and sometimes it was sold in the local meat market (10:25). Many pagan temples, including some of those excavated in Corinth, had dining facilities where worshipers could banquet on the remains from the sacrifice. In most cases, these were not "religious meals" as such, but social occasions, not unlike many church suppers enjoyed by Christians today.

Paul Refused to Settle for Simplistic Answers

As usual when dealing with moral issues Paul refused to settle for simplistic answers. Taking particular circumstances into account, he qualified his views accordingly. In the present case he considered four different sets of circumstances. Three of these were mentioned only near the end of his discussion. What about buying meat from the public market? Christians could do so without questioning its origin (10:25). What if a Christian was invited to dinner in the home of a pagan relative or friend? Again, one need not worry about the origin of the meat (10:27). What if, on such an occasion, someone volunteered the information that the meat had come from a pagan temple? In that case, Paul said, the Christian guest(s) should decline to eat it (10:28-29).

Apparently, some members of the Corinthian church believed there was nothing wrong with eating meat from pagan temples. Others, perhaps, were either hesitant to eat it or specifically opposed eating it. As a result, Paul identified the issues as he saw them, and offered his opinion about what course of action was most authentically Christian.

What was Paul's theological foundation for his comments in chapter 10? They can be found primarily in chapter 8, where yet another situation was in view. There the question was whether Christians could join pagan relatives and friends in the banquets that took place in temple dining rooms. Even as he introduced this topic (8:1-6), Paul began reasoning his way toward an answer.

The apostle began by quoting those who supported eating temple meat. In defense of their position they claimed that "all of us possess knowledge" (8:1a). The reference is to knowing that the gods pagans worship do not really exist, because "there is no God but one" (4). This claim echoes the most basic affirmation of Jewish faith, taken from Deuteronomy 6:4, that "The Lord is our God, the Lord alone" (NRSV, see footnote). Paul, like all Christians, affirmed this knowledge about God. Nonetheless, he qualified the Corinthians' claim in several ways. For one thing, he did not rule out absolutely the existence of "so-called" gods and lords, only their significance "for us" (5-6). However, his most important qualifications of the claim about knowledge occur in verses 1b-3 and verse 6.

Knowledge *About* God Versus Knowledge *of* God

In verses 1b-3 Paul made an important distinction between knowledge about God and knowledge of God. The distinction becomes clear when we consider ways of knowing people. Knowledge about a person can be gained secondhand—for example, from newspapers or television. However, knowledge of a person requires the kind of experience or involvement that comes only through a personal relationship. The Corinthians proudly claimed to "know something" about God, whereas Paul emphasized that the "necessary knowledge" was of a different order: a knowledge of God that derived from an actual relationship with God.

Paul described the relationship through which this "necessary knowledge" was established and sustained as God's "knowledge" of us (8:3). Here the apostle was employing Old Testament language (for example, Exodus 33:12, 17; Jeremiah 1:5) to speak of God's gracious love by which women and men are formed into God's own people (see also Romans 8:29-30).

Paul Adapted a Statement of Faith

A further qualification of the Corinthians' claim to knowledge is implicit in the two-part affirmation of 1 Corinthians 8:6. The first part affirms that there is "one God, the Father," who is both the ground and goal of all creation, including humankind. Here Paul incorporated the Corinthians' claim to knowledge about one God, but went beyond that to speak of God's relationship to creation. The second part of the statement affirmed that there is also "one Lord, Jesus Christ," who is God's agent for the creation of "all things" and for our human existence in particular.

> Paul's elegant phrasing suggests that Paul may have adapted a statement of faith that had been circulated and used in Christian circles for some time.

This having been affirmed, Paul proceeded with his counsels about eating meat that had been ritually slaughtered in pagan temples. The Corinthians' knowledge about "one God, the Father" is only part of the basis on which they were to decide the question. Above all, they were to be guided by the character of their relationship to God, as they had come to experience that through their "one Lord, Jesus Christ."

Love Is More Important Than Knowledge

Paul's advice was based on a line of reasoning that could be summed up in five points.

- In principle, Christians have a "right" or "liberty" (9, NRSV) to eat meat from pagan sacrifices, because they know that there is but one God.
- However, not all Christians are fully enough enlightened about God. Being "weak" in their knowledge, they continue to suppose that pagan sacrifices have some meaning (7).
- If these "weak" Christians are influenced by the example of other Christians to eat the meat, they might—in their own minds—be violating their commitment to the gospel (10).
- What nourishes faith is not our knowledge about God, but that Christ died for us, revealing God's love. As recipients of this love, believers are also revealed to one another as sisters and brothers in God's family (11).
- To sin against any member of this family is to sin against Christ himself (12).

57

This is the line of thought that led Paul to the conclusion he stated first in verse 9, then again in verse 13. Love, he said, is always more important than knowledge, and rights always involve responsibilities. Therefore, whenever the exercise of one's rights, however legitimate, might endanger the well-being of a brother or sister, those rights are to be given up. For Paul, this "giving up" in no way diminishes us, either as Christians or as human beings. Rather, as an expression of God's love working through us, this particular kind of "giving up" represents the fulfillment of our highest calling in Christ—and therefore, as human beings.

Dimension 3:
What Does the Bible Mean to Us?

Where Is the Relevance?

Most Christians today have no reason to worry about whether they should be eating meat that has been left over from pagan rites! It is therefore understandable if readers are tempted to skip Paul's discussion of this matter, and move quickly to some other passage that appears to be more relevant. However, some second thoughts are in order.

Multiculturalism raises issues for the modern church that are comparable, at least generally, to the issue addressed by Paul in 1 Corinthians 8. Therefore, the apostle's word to his church in Corinth is, at least generally, still on target for the church today. It summons us to be considerate and supportive of persons whose experience of Christ, commitment to the gospel, and understanding of the Christian life have been shaped by cultural traditions and forces different from our own.

To begin with, in parts of the world where Christianity is a minority religion and drawing converts from other religions, somewhat comparable situations still occur. Has the church an obligation to discourage all members from practices that some new converts may continue to associate with religious beliefs they have supposedly given up? Where such questions have to be asked, Paul's counsel will seem less remote than where Christians have little contact with other religions or converts from them.

Moreover, even where Christians may never know a convert from another religion, the church today must respond to the challenges and opportunities that are presented by a multicultural society.

The Passage Commands Attention

Quite beyond these points, however, there are several general features of this passage that command our attention and invite reflection.

Paul's entire discussion presupposes that Christ's death is both the demonstration of God's love and definitive for how God's love is to be known in Christian community. In this passage, as throughout Paul's letters, we are reminded that what Christians do is to be governed by who they are in Christ. The significance of this fact is more apparent when we note two appeals that Paul *did not make* to the Corinthians.

On the one hand, he did not appeal to them to be guided by their individual "consciences" or experiences of the Spirit. In 1 Corinthians 8:1–11:1, *conscience* is described mainly in negative terms, as "weak," illinformed, and not to be relied on (8:7, 10, 12; 10:25, 27-29). The Spirit is not mentioned at all in this part of the letter. Paul knew that conscience cannot be a norm, because it is subject to one's individual experiences, knowledge, and beliefs. It may therefore fluctuate between "strong" and "weak." He also knew, from dealing with the Corinthians, that claims about "having the Spirit" are sometimes only claims about one's particular "religious" experience. Any such claim, like any appeal to conscience, must always be tested by reference to the norm of the gospel.

On the other hand, Paul also did not invoke any church rule about meat that came from pagan temples. A rule about this does appear elsewhere in the New Testament. According to Acts 15:1-29, Paul himself had been party to an agreement, reached in Jerusalem some years before he wrote 1 Corinthians, that Gentile converts must "abstain . . . from things polluted by idols" (Acts 15:20). This certainly included meat from pagan rites (see also Revelation 2:14). But for Paul, every rule, like every experience of the Spirit, was to be tested by reference to the norm of the gospel, which is God's love as revealed in Christ, especially in Christ's death.

This passage shows that Christian calculations about "right" and "wrong" must always take account of more than just the bare act, what is done or not done. As Paul saw it, neither eating nor declining to eat meat from pagan temples was in itself either good or bad (8:8b). Especially from a Christian viewpoint, moral judgments must be based on an assessment of motives, intentions, and consequences, including the effects of an action on other people.

The Importance of Personal Example

First Corinthians 8 also draws our attention to the importance of personal example in shaping the moral life of individuals and communities. On the negative side, Paul feared that if knowledgeable Christians ate in pagan temples, their example might be followed by the less knowledgeable, who would then be violating convictions from which they were not yet fully liberated (8:10).

Finally, this passage prompts us to reflect on two matters that the apostle himself was apparently not thinking about when he wrote it.

Being sensitive and accommodating to the situation of those who appear to be "weak" in faith is only a first step. The church's larger objective

Paul offered his own practice as a positive example—indirectly in 8:13 (he himself would never eat meat lest others be harmed) and chapter 9 (he himself had given up "rights"), then quite directly in 10:32–11:1, to conclude his whole discussion: the Corinthians should imitate him just as he has imitated Christ, by setting aside self-interest in order to save others.

must be to strengthen the faith of every believer through an ongoing process of Christian formation (including "Christian education"). Paul seemed not to have conceived of such a process, probably because he assumed that there would not be enough time to carry it out before Christ's return. However, our situation is different. Supporting those who are less knowledgeable about the gospel and less experienced in the Christian life must include helping them grow in their understanding and mature in their faith.

Sometimes Christian love requires that accommodation take the form of dialogue, or even confrontation. Giving up one's "right" to eat meat from pagan temples didn't require giving up anything that was vital for faith. But what if the integrity of the gospel itself is at stake, or if equally well-informed Christians hold differing views? In such cases, Christian love calls for respectful dialogue, the courage to stand firm in positions that are based on sound evidence and clear reasoning, and a readiness to abandon positions that are shown to be uninformed or ill-considered.

Dimension 4: A Daily Bible Journey Plan

Day 1: 1 Corinthians 12:1-13

Day 2: 1 Corinthians 12:14-31

Day 3: 1 Corinthians 13:1-13

Day 4: 1 Corinthians 14:1-19

Day 5: 1 Corinthians 14:20-40

Day 6: 1 Corinthians 15:1-23

Day 7: 1 Corinthians 15:24-34

1 Corinthians 12:4-27

8

FAITH, INCORPORATED

What to Watch For

Read at least 1 Corinthians 12:4-27. You may also wish to read all of chapters 12 through 14.

Paul portrayed the church as "the body of Christ" (1 Corinthians 12:27). He compared the individual members of this faith community with the parts of a human body. In making the comparison, he emphasized that both diversity and unity characterize a properly functioning body.

To appreciate the full significance of this passage, pay attention first to its setting in chapter 12. In this chapter, Paul began a discussion of spiritual gifts (see 12:1). His comments about the diversity of gifts and the body of Christ helped to establish the foundation for everything that follows in chapters 12 and 13, and especially for the appeals and specific directives in chapter 14.

This passage makes a number of important affirmations. Note what the apostle said about the following:

➤ God's intention in constituting the Christian community with different kinds of members;
➤ the Spirit;
➤ baptism;
➤ how the body's "weaker" members are to be regarded;
➤ what happens when any one member of the body suffers or is honored.

1. Why has each person been given some kind of spiritual gift?

2. What nine "manifestations of the Spirit" did Paul mention in the focus passage (1 Corinthians 12:4-27)?

3. What did Paul say about "the head" of the body?

4. Which members of the body are treated with special respect?

The Christians of Corinth were especially proud of their spiritual gifts. Paul himself acknowledged that they "are not lacking in any spiritual gift" (1 Corinthians 1:7). But he also knew that competition to display certain coveted gifts was contributing to the tensions within his congregation. He therefore devoted a major part of First Corinthians to the topic (see "An Outline of 1 Corinthians 11:2–14:40").

The apostle opened his discussion by emphasizing in 1 Corinthians 12:4-11:

- the diversity of spiritual gifts;
- that every believer has been granted some gift;
- that they are equally the Spirit's gifts;
- that God has granted them for a specific purpose.

AN OUTLINE OF 1 CORINTHIANS 11:2–14:40 (COUNSELS ABOUT LIFE WITHIN THE CHURCH)

Introductory commendation	11:2
Women who pray or prophesy	11:3-16
Disorders at the Lord's Supper	11:17-34
Spiritual gifts	12:1–14:40
Introduction: speaking by the Spirit	12:1-3
The body of Christ	12:4–13:13
The diversity of gifts	12:4-11
The body and its members	12:12-31a
The most excellent way of love	12:31b–13:13
Appeals and directives	14:1-36
The primary appeal: pursue love	14:1-12
A secondary appeal: think like adults	14:13-25
Directives for the assembly	14:26-36
Conclusion: a call for order	14:37-40

Paul feared that these points had been forgotten, perhaps even disputed, by the Corinthians. They supposed that a person's spiritual gift showed how "spiritual" she or he was. Speaking in tongues, one of the more spectacular gifts, was especially prized. Those who displayed it enjoyed a privileged status within the congregation.

The Diversity of Spiritual Gifts

Paul was not against speaking in tongues. In chapter 14 he expressed the wish that all believers could have this gift (14:5). He claimed that he himself spoke in tongues more than anyone in Corinth (14:18). However, these were incidental remarks, and possibly exaggerations. His main points were (1) that one need not speak in tongues, and (2) that other gifts, especially prophesying, were more important—not in themselves, but for "building up" the congregation (see 14:1-5, 13-19). Paul gave the theological basis for these judgments in chapters 12 and 13.

Paul emphasized, first, the diversity of the Spirit's gifts (12:4). The Corinthians needed to learn that speaking in tongues was but one gift among many. In fact, Paul seemed intentionally to put "tongues" and "the interpretation of tongues" at the bottom of the list (12:8-10, 28, 29-30). (See "Spiritual Gifts," page 64.)

SPIRITUAL GIFTS

There are six different listings of spiritual gifts in the New Testament. Four are in letters that were certainly written by Paul (1 Corinthians 12:8-10; 12:28; 12:29-30; Romans 12:6-8), one in a letter attributed to Paul but probably not written by him (Ephesians 4:11), and one in a letter attributed to Peter (1 Peter 4:10-11). No two lists are identical, although there is some overlapping.

Paul's four lists, taken together, mention seventeen different gifts. Prophecy is the only one that appears in all four. Christian prophets were persons who, on certain occasions, conveyed an oracle or saying that they attributed to God, the Spirit, or the resurrected Jesus. Ordinarily, these prophecies concerned the present, although some were about Christ's expected return.

Three of Paul's lists mention healing, working miracles, and speaking in tongues. Tongue-speaking consisted of ecstatic utterances that were intelligible only to those who had a gift for interpreting tongues. This gift of interpretation and the gift of apostleship are included in two of Paul's four lists.

Most of the spiritual gifts identified by Paul are listed just once. Wisdom and knowledge, gifts especially favored in Corinth, are named only in 1 Corinthians 12:8-10, as are the gifts of wonder-working "faith" (different from the faith that justifies) and discernment of spirits (evaluating statements that Christian prophets claim to be inspired). The gifts of assisting and giving guidance appear only in 1 Corinthians 12:28, and the gifts of serving, encouraging, sharing, leading, and doing acts of mercy appear only in Romans 12:6-8.

Derived From the Same Spirit

Paul also registered his conviction that "everyone" (12:6b)—"each" person (12:7, 11)—was graced with some gift. Perhaps the Corinthians were denying this. At the least, they seemed to be honoring as truly "spiritual" only those members of their congregation who displayed the more spectacular gifts. This, too, concerned Paul, and led him to stress another point.

In saying, repeatedly, that every spiritual gift came from "the same Spirit" (12:4, 8, 9, 11), he emphasized that the kind of gift one has was less important than its source. However modest the gift, it still derived from "the same Spirit." Therefore, it gave the recipient equal standing with every other member of the congregation. The Corinthians needed to stop judging one's faith on the basis of the kind of gift that one could display.

Paul's statement about why the Spirit grants these gifts is also important. The Corinthians wanted to have gifts that would benefit them most as individuals. In their congregation, anyone fortunate enough to have had a supposedly better gift enjoyed greater respect and had higher standing than those who had received some less-valued gift. According to Paul, however, spiritual gifts were granted "for the common good" (12:7), to benefit the believing community as a whole. This objective of "building up the church" (14:3-5, 12, 17, 26) led the apostle himself to identify some gifts as "greater" than others (12:31; 14:5). But it also demanded that he replace the Corinthian criterion of self-interest with the test of love. Love is what "builds up" (see 8:1) both individuals and communities, because love looks beyond self-interest to the interests of others (see 12:31b–13:13).

The apostle illustrated and amplified these points by likening the church to a human body (12:12-13). Just as the separate parts of a body comprise an organic whole, so individual believers are one in Christ. Baptism is the sign and seal of this new reality. In baptism, through "the one Spirit," all believers—no matter what their ethnic or social status—have become "one body" (see "A Baptismal Affirmation"). Their diversity remains but now finds expression in their unity.

A BAPTISMAL AFFIRMATION

Paul's words in 1 Corinthians 12:13 echo an affirmation of faith that was perhaps used in services of baptism. This same affirmation lies behind Colossians 3:10-11. It is preserved in a more original form in Galatians 3:27-28. By comparing 1 Corinthians 12:13 with the other two passages, we can see how Paul tailored the traditional affirmation to fit the Corinthian situation.

First, because Paul's overall topic was spiritual gifts, he added a reference to the Spirit's role in baptism. Neither of the parallel statements mentioned the Spirit at all.

Second, he worked in a reference to the "body," which, like the Spirit, he described as "one." Neither parallel statement employed the body image, and neither was as explicit about the unity that baptism represented.

Third, in First Corinthians Paul mentioned the unity only of Jews and Greeks and of slaves and free. He omitted the reference to "male" and "female" that was part of the earlier form in Galatians. This omission could have been accidental. If it was deliberate, there is no telling why. Either way, Paul did not mean to retract his view, evident elsewhere in this letter, that men and women, too, are one in Christ.

Portrayed as a Body

As Paul proceeded with his portrayal of the church as a body (12:14-27), four additional points stand out.

> This body was not like a band of shipwrecked strangers, bound together only by the predicament they shared. This body was constituted by the gift of life, not by the threat of death.

- He did not identify Christ as "head" of the body. It was otherwise in Ephesians and Colossians, where Christ was indeed affirmed to be the "head" of the church. But here (and in Romans 12:4-5), Christ was associated with the body in its entirety (27).

- The members of Christ's body were described as existing for one another, and thus for the body as a whole. They were fully interdependent, serving and caring for one another (15-17, 19-21, 25), and sharing in one another's sufferings, honors, and joys (verse 26).

- It was by God's express intent, not by happenstance, that Christ's body was composed of diverse, interdependent members (18, 24b).

- Paul stressed that the "weaker" and "less honorable" (respectable) members of Christ's body were also indispensable (22-24).

Dimension 3: What Does the Bible Mean to Us?

How Are You Graced by the Spirit?

Our focus passage can deepen our understanding both of spiritual gifts and of the church.

We are alerted, first, to the diversity of the Spirit's gifts. The Corinthians had been preoccupied with just one—speaking in tongues.

> It is also important to affirm, with Paul, that nobody has been left without at least one kind of spiritual gift.

This is a preoccupation in some modern congregations, too. In such cases the apostle's correctives can be applied fairly directly. More often, though, we neglect to honor the diversity of gifts by presuming that all "good Christians" must devote their time and energies to roughly the same array of church activities. Paul, however, never offered a standard profile of "the good church member." Because the Spirit's gifts are diverse, there are varied patterns of Christian service.

We neglect to honor this diversity if we suppose that spiritual gifts are only those particular "gifts and graces" that qualify a person for the church's ordained or professional ministries. As a result, people who lack these qualifying gifts may fail to recognize and use their own special gifts. When this happens, it is a loss both to them and to the church.

For believers, the question is not whether one has been graced by the Spirit but how. Then the question becomes how one's gifts can best be nourished, developed, and employed. One of our important tasks in the church is to assist one another in identifying and using the gifts that have been distributed among us.

No "Second-Class" Gifts

In attending to these spiritual gifts, we must take care not to assume that some are inherently better than others. One's gifts are no indication of one's standing with God, and they are not to be the basis for one's standing in the church. For example, it is no higher a calling to be a member of the clergy than a member of the choir, or no less a calling to care for a church building than for the people who come there to worship, learn, and organize for service in the world.

> There are no "second-class" gifts and no "second-class" Christians.

Indeed, our passage also shows us that service is the purpose for which the Spirit's gifts are bestowed. They are to be employed for "the common good." When, like the Corinthians, we use them only to further our own good we are abusing them. Just as it is a loss to ourselves and others when we neglect our gifts, so it is an offense to the Spirit when we use them to advance ourselves over others.

Love—the "Most Excellent Way"

For this reason Paul stressed that love is "the most excellent way" (1 Corinthians 13). Significantly, he did not list it as one of the Spirit's "gifts." He called it, rather, the first and all-inclusive "fruit" of the Spirit (Galatians 5:22). God's love affirms and claims all of us, not just some. Love also affirms our gifts, by claiming all of them "for the common good."

How this works is shown by Paul's description of the church as Christ's body. Ancient physicians knew nothing about the critical importance of the circulatory system for a body's functioning. Otherwise, the apostle could have identified love as the vital life force that courses through the veins and arteries of Christ's body, keeping it vital and flourishing. This idea is implicit, nonetheless, in his emphasis on the interdependence of the body's members. Life in Christ means living for one another.

"Faith, Inc."

Beyond this, Paul's description of the body of Christ suggests several points at which we may need to rethink our understanding of the church:
● The church is not a mere association of people who happen to share similar life experiences, needs, hopes, or values. The identity and unity of the church does not derive from its members, but from the God of Jesus

67

Christ by whom we have been graced with love and claimed for love's work. We may think of the church as "Faith, Inc.," a community of believers "in-corporated" as Christ's body.

- In worship, we celebrate whose and who we are by reaffirming our life in Christ, listening for the word of God, and rededicating ourselves to lives of faithful service.

- This worshiping community—"Faith, Inc."—has been constituted as a "not-for-profit" corporation. We all recognize the obvious sense in which this idea is true. However, our passage alerts us to a deeper sense in which it is true. The church does not exist to bring even spiritual "profits" to its corporate partners and certainly not to perpetuate or enhance itself as an institution. The partners of this corporation already share fully in the "profits" of God's love in Christ. Nothing the church can do will either increase or decrease this treasury of grace. Its mission is to manifest God's grace in its corporate life and to equip all of the partners to do the same in their individual lives.

> Nothing a congregation does is as important as its corporate worship of God.

- Those who may appear to be the weakest, most vulnerable, or least respectable partners in this corporation are to be accorded special honor. This way is not the world's way, and usually not the church's way either. This way makes no sense if the church exists to enhance its own or its members' standing in the world. But if the church exists to give God's love a presence in the world, it is the only way. The church honors its "needy" members (not "inferior," as in the NRSV translation of 12:24) by ministering to them in their need, and also by laboring to deliver them from it.

Dimension 4:
A Daily Bible Journey Plan

Day 1: 1 Corinthians 15:35-58

Day 2: 1 Corinthians 16:1-12

Day 3: 1 Corinthians 16:13-24

Day 4: 2 Corinthians 1:1-22

Day 5: 2 Corinthians 1:23–2:13

Day 6: 2 Corinthians 2:14–3:18

Day 7: 2 Corinthians 4:1-15

2 Corinthians 5:12–6:2

9

A NEW CREATION

What to Watch For

Read 2 Corinthians 5:12–6:2. This passage includes the closing paragraphs of Paul's comments about apostleship and a few verses from the closely related appeals to which his comments led. Without question, what Paul said here about apostleship applies in a general way also to every Christian. Nonetheless, the force of his words will be lost if we do not recognize that they are directed, in the first instance, to questions that had been raised about the validity of his own ministry.

The main theme in these verses is reconciliation. Paul used this term in three connections:

➤ as he affirmed God's "reconciling" work in Christ;
➤ as he wrote of his own "ministry of reconciliation";
➤ as he appealed to his Corinthian congregation to "be reconciled with God."

In addition, our passage includes several statements about the saving significance of Christ's death and important declarations about the already present reality of "a new creation" and "the day of salvation."

1. For whom did Christ die, and with what result?

2. What is the dramatically new situation for those who are "in Christ"?

3. In this passage, Paul attributed four or five different actions or functions to Christ. Can you find at least three of these?

4. *Reconciliation* is a key word in this passage. According to Paul, who needs to be reconciled to whom, and who takes the initiative in bringing this about?

Dimension 2:
What Does the Bible Mean?

Paul's Apostleship Questioned

According to a number of scholars, the first nine chapters of the writing we know as "Second Corinthians" are from a letter that is at least the fourth in sequence of Paul's letters to his church in Corinth. In the earlier "First Corinthians" some hints already show that certain unnamed members of that congregation were beginning to question Paul's apostolic standing. By the time Paul wrote Second Corinthians, criticism of him seems to have been on the rise. Rival apostles (who they were, we do not know) had arrived in Corinth. They sought to discredit Paul by suggesting that he wasn't "religious" enough, successful enough in his ministry, or well enough "connected" to important figures in the church.

These outsiders had apparently brought with them letters of recommendation, which was customary in the ancient world. The letters presumably showed that these people had "good connections," perhaps with the leaders of the church in Jerusalem. This action prompted Paul to say that he himself had never needed such letters; the Corinthians' own faith demonstrated that his ministry had been authorized by God, not simply by church officials (2 Corinthians 3:1-5).

For his part, Paul regarded his rivals as mere "peddlers of God's word," out for self-gain and not sincerely devoted to serving the gospel (2:17). Nonetheless, Paul still felt that their demeaning of his apostleship required some response. We find this response in 2 Corinthians 1–9, especially in 2:14–5:19. This is the principal context for understanding this session's focus passage. (See "An Outline of 2 Corinthians 1–9.")

AN OUTLINE OF 2 CORINTHIANS 1–9

Letter opening	1:1-2
Blessing	1:3-11
Assurances, instruction, warnings	1:12–9:15
Assurances of concern	1:12–2:13
Comments on apostolic service	2:14–5:19
Introduction	2:14–3:6
The ministry of the new covenant	3:7–4:6
The ministry and mortality	4:7–5:10
The ministry of reconciliation	5:11-19
Various appeals and warnings	5:20–9:15
Reconciliation with God	5:20–6:10
Reconciliation with Paul	6:11–7:3
The collection for Jerusalem	7:4–9:15

Paul Responded to Critics

In 2 Corinthians 5:12-13 Paul responded to two specific criticisms:
● Someone had charged that because Paul had no letters of reference from notable people, he had to resort to recommending himself.
● Someone also criticized Paul for not being as deeply religious as the rival apostles. Unlike rival apostles, he was not noted for public displays of religious ecstasy, which people in Corinth, both Christians and pagans, valued highly.

Paul responded by assuring his readers that he wished only to help them know how to answer his detractors (5:12). In addition (5:13), he identified ecstatic experiences—being "beside oneself"—as individual and private, between oneself and God; such experiences were of no benefit to others. Instead, constructive actions and intelligible speech—being in one's "right mind"—benefitted others. The aim and mode of his apostleship was only to live, preach, and interpret the gospel in ways that other people would understand and be changed. He had spelled out this same view in an earlier letter when he commended the rational speech of "prophesying" as more beneficial to the church than the unintelligible sounds of "speaking in tongues" (1 Corinthians 12–14).

Christ Died for Our Sins

In making these points, Paul could not resist a counterthrust at his rivals. They were "those who boast in outward appearance and not in the heart" (5:12). "Outward appearance" was first of all a reference to the dramatic religious seizures of which those rivals were so proud. The apostle might also be thinking of the displays of flowery speech with which ancient audiences liked to be entertained, but which Paul himself avoided (see 1 Corinthians 2:1-5; 2 Corinthians 10:10; 11:6).

In its traditional form, the statement, "Christ died for our sins," suggests that for our sins Christ took upon himself the penalty that we deserve.

Christ's love, which had embraced and claimed his life (5:14a), impelled and energized his ministry, Paul said. The defining event of this love was Christ's self-giving on the cross, to which the apostle referred in 5:14b-15. Behind this reference lay an affirmation of faith that had already attained creedlike status among Christian congregations: "Christ died for our sins" (for example, 1 Corinthians 15:3). Christ therefore died in our place that we might live. A similar view surfaces in 5:21, in the comment that God brought about an exchange of humanity's sin and Christ's righteousness.

Delivered From the Tyranny of Self-Interest

Paul, however, offered a bold new interpretation of this traditional "substitutionary" belief. Instead of saying that Christ had died for all that all might live, he said that Christ had died for all that all might die!

Paul explained what he meant in 5:15:

- Those who respond to the gospel with faith ("who live") are delivered from the tyranny of narrow self-interest (living "for themselves") that diminishes their humanity. Elsewhere Paul expressed this as a dying to self (Galatians 2:19-20), or the death of the "old self" (Romans 6:6-7).
- In Christ (living "for him"; see also Romans 6:8) those who respond to the gospel with faith are delivered over to a life for others that enlarges and enriches their humanity. The power of this new life is the power of love, demonstrated in Christ's death and affirmed in his resurrection.

In 5:16 Paul mentioned Christ again, but only to illustrate a more specific point: those who are in Christ should no longer regard people "from a human point of view." Paul himself had once so regarded Christ. The apostle was still thinking of those who judged his ministry according to "outward appearance" (5:12), and called it inadequate because he provided no religious or oratorical displays. His own change of viewpoint about Christ probably involved his interpretation of Christ's death: before he accepted the gospel, he had regarded the cross as a problem (see 1 Corinthians 1:23); now he proclaimed it as defining God's love (2 Corinthians 5:14a; Romans 5:8).

The idea of an eventual new creation had Old Testament roots (see, especially, Isaiah 65:17-25). Subsequently, this prominent idea appeared in Jewish "apocalyptic" writings, so described because they presented "revelations" about what God would do in the future.

Paul's declaration in 5:17 about "a new creation" both gathered up and undergirded what he had been saying in verses 14-16. However, Paul affirmed that the new creation had already occurred through Christ. He did not simply mean that individual believers are made new in Christ. He believed this, of course; but his vision was cosmic in scope. He was affirming a whole new order of creation. Everything old had been replaced, even though not yet destroyed; its destruction would come only at "the end" (1 Corinthians 15:24-28).

The Difference Between Old and New

As Paul saw it, the rule of God's love that has been instituted in Christ's death (5:14-15) marks the difference between the old and the new. If this new order of creation appears only to those who see with the eyes of faith, it is no less real. However, the new creation becomes visible even in a "public" sense—for all the world to see and experience—where the rule of love is given an active, working presence within the community of faith and in the lives of its members.

Reconciliation—God's Gift

The remainder of our focus passage extends the discussion of this new creation by introducing the idea of *reconciliation* (5:18–6:2). Here, as in 5:14-15, Paul's language seems to echo a creed: "In Christ God was reconciling the world to himself, not counting their trespasses against them" (5:19). Humankind has alienated itself from God by violating the terms on which that relationship is founded. However, Paul did not say that God needs to be "appeased" somehow and "won back" to caring about the world! Paul's point, which he had already expressed in his own words in 5:18a, identified Christ as God's agent in the work of reconciliation.

The metaphor of "reconciliation" (see also Romans 5:10-11; Ephesians 2:16; Colossians 1:20, 22) presents God's work in Christ as the restoring of a relationship that has been broken off. By turning from God, "the world" has alienated itself from the source of its life. In Christ, God has reached out in love to embrace the world and give it new life. The metaphor of "reconciliation" conveys with special appropriateness the apostle's conviction that the gospel is about the renewal of relationships through the nurturing presence of a "love that will not let us go."

> True apostles engage in "the ministry of reconciliation" (5:18b) and proclaim "the message of reconciliation" (5:19b).

Paul wanted the Corinthians to understand that this gospel of reconciliation defined his apostleship. Whatever else his critics might say about the requirements for apostleship, the one critical matter was whether God's reconciling love found expression in Paul's ministry.

Finally, if the gospel of reconciliation defined Paul's apostleship, then so it also defined the Corinthians' faith. Paul spoke to them on Christ's behalf, appealing to them to "be reconciled to God" (5:20). The apostle was in no way qualifying what he had just affirmed, that reconciliation had already taken place through Christ (5:18-19); reconciliation remained God's gift. However, reconciliation is a gift that must be received; God's grace must be accepted and allowed to show in one's life (see 6:1).

Dimension 3:
What Does the Bible Mean to Us?

The Great Importance of Relationships

Our passage commands attention because of what it says about the ministry and message of reconciliation, and how the transforming power of Christ's love finds expression in the Christian life. These closely related themes connect in Paul's vision of "a new creation."

The metaphor of "reconciliation" indicates that the gospel is essentially about relationships. Fundamentally, it concerns humankind's relationship with God. According to Paul, this relationship is founded on God's love as expressed in Christ's death "for all." In this sense, Christ is the agent through whom God's reconciling work takes place.

Second, Paul's gospel of reconciliation concerns our relationships with other people. As persons reconciled with God, we have both the possibility and responsibility of being reconciled with one another.

What is the character of the reconciling love that constitutes the gospel by and to which we are called? Several specific characteristics of this kind of love emerge in the course of Paul's remarks:

● Love that genuinely and powerfully reconciles is not incidental to a relationship but integral to it. Such love cannot sometimes be given and sometimes withheld, depending on the circumstances. This does not mean that reconciling love is "blind" to circumstances, or indifferent to the presence of evil or injustice. It takes account of circumstances and opposes evil and injustice—but not by withholding love itself. Although love does not "count up" trespasses, it nonetheless names them as such—precisely in order to deal with them redemptively, in ways that can restore and sustain the relationship.

• Genuinely reconciling love is universal in its scope. It knows no boundaries, it embraces "the world," it is "for all." To set limits on love's extent would be to set limits on God and to diminish love's power. Love's circle has a center in the gracious *yes* of God's affirming presence; and this center holds. But love's circle has no perimeters, because God's yes extends endlessly outward, embracing the whole of creation, and never asking, "How far?"

• Reconciling love enlarges and enriches our lives by freeing us to live for others. In Paul's words, Christ's love impels us to live no longer for ourselves but for him (5:15); and to live for Christ means to live under the rule of his love. We therefore live in company with "all" for whom Christ died.

We live for ourselves when we remain indifferent to those near or far who are the victims of injustice, oppression, warfare, economic exploitation, or natural disaster; but surely no less when self-interest and personal ambition are allowed to govern our lives.

> Only in community, in our life together, do we flourish as human beings.

We live for others when we accept and affirm them as children of God, no less than ourselves; when we join with them to seek and support the common good; and when we aid them in their time of need. Living for others does not diminish us but fulfills us.

Love's rule in Christ lays claim to us in a way that commands, but does not coerce, the response of faith. This point must be carefully understood. On the one hand, God's love for us is real and present whether we respond in faith or not. As the poet, Francis Thompson, expressed it, although "human love needs human meriting," God's love "pursues" us, despite our unworthiness and fearful flight, "down the nights and down the days" of our lives; and "Fear wist not to evade as Love wist to pursue." (From "The Hound of Heaven")

God's Love Invites Faith

On the other hand, God's reconciling love does not become real for us until we allow its transforming power to be shown in our lives and to have a concrete presence in the place that we inhabit. But even though love lays total claim to our lives, it cannot compel us to respond in faith. If it did, it would lose its character as love. Faith would lose its character as a response. We could not then speak of genuine "reconciliation." Therefore,

God's love "invites" faith, and where the invitation is accepted, the believer becomes an agent of reconciling love.

This point may be illustrated by a remarkable, true story coming out of World War II. When American forces retook the Pacific island of Guam, one Japanese soldier, a Sergeant Yokoi, escaped capture by fleeing into the mountains. There he remained for 28 years, isolated from the outside world. When he finally emerged from hiding, on January 24, 1972, the war had been long concluded and the United States and Japan, formerly enemies, were now friends.

For Sergeant Yokoi, however, this was news. He was confronted with a reconciliation that had changed the world. In a political sense, there had been "a new creation" while he was in the mountains. However, it remained for him to accept this new reality, to allow it to transform his life and inhabit the place where he was. Doing so demanded a radically new self-understanding, a fundamental reordering of his relationships with other people, and a thorough reassessment of the commitments, priorities, and goals that he had been taking for granted. "You have been reconciled; therefore be reconciled." This was the word he needed to hear.

Similarly, the gospel summons us to embrace the reconciliation that is already given, but that must also be given a place in our lives. This can happen only in concrete and practical ways: in our relationships with family, friends, and fellow workers; in our role as citizens of local communities, and beyond; and by no means least, in the church, which has been entrusted in special ways with the ministry and message of God's reconciling love in Christ.

Dimension 4:
A Daily Bible Journey Plan

Day 1: 2 Corinthians 4:16–5:10

Day 2: 2 Corinthians 5:11–6:2

Day 3: 2 Corinthians 6:3–7:1

Day 4: 2 Corinthians 7:2-16

Day 5: 2 Corinthians 8:1-24

Day 6: 2 Corinthians 9:1-15

Day 7: 2 Corinthians 10:1-18

10

STRENGTH THROUGH WEAKNESS

What to Watch For

This passage is often described as "a fool's speech" because of the way that Paul himself seems to have thought of what he was saying. He was talking like a fool, and he knew it. He emphasized it (see 11:1, 21b; 12:11). He felt compelled to speak in this manner because of the sharp criticisms of his apostleship that circulated in the Corinthian congregation. To counteract the pretentious claims of certain rival apostles, he made some claims of his own.

As Paul made his claims, we learn some fascinating things about his life, both past and present. He wrote of the following:

➤ his Jewishness;
➤ the hardships and dangers that had plagued his ministry;
➤ a long-ago ecstatic experience;
➤ some kind of troublesome "thorn in the flesh."

However, we should not become distracted by these fascinating glimpses into Paul's life. Notice instead that Paul identified all of these experiences as "weaknesses," and that he interpreted them in accord with a word about "grace" that he had received from the Lord.

1. Paul catalogued more than twenty different hardships that he had to endure as an apostle. How many can you find?

2. What danger had Paul faced in Damascus, and what was his response to it?

3. What was Paul's explanation for the affliction that he described as "a thorn in the flesh"?

4. Paul prayed repeatedly for relief from his "thorn in the flesh." What happened in response to his prayers?

Dimension 2:
What Does the Bible Mean?

Paul's main concern in 2 Corinthians 10–13 was to save his Corinthian congregation from being taken over by some rival apostles. (Read about "Paul's Rivals" in the box.)

PAUL'S RIVALS

In Second Corinthians Paul contrasted his ministry with that of certain rival apostles who were trying to take charge of the Corinthian church. These persons were never named by Paul; his Corinthian readers would know very well to whom he was referring. We today are left to catch whatever glimpses of them we can by reading between the lines. Although the picture that emerges is not completely in focus, it still gives us some idea of what the apostle was up against.

- Evidently more than one person was involved (see 10:2, 12; 11:12-13). Whether more than two or three rivals were involved, we do not know.
- These people had come to Corinth from somewhere else (11:4), and were Jewish Christians (11:22), like Paul himself.
- The rivals must have claimed to be apostles, because Paul described them as "false apostles" (11:13) and—sarcastically—"super-apostles" (11:5;

12:11). Many of his other references to them are at least as negative: for example, "deceitful workers" (11:13), Satan's ministers in disguise (11:14-15), and "fools" (11:19).
- These people carried with them letters of recommendation (3:1)—from where or whom, we do not know. In addition, they did not hesitate to boast about their own status and accomplishments as "ministers of Christ" (11:23; see also 5:12; 10:12; 11:12, 18).
- They coupled their self-commendation with sharp criticism of Paul. They charged him with being weak and ineffectual, as well as ill-mannered in speech (10:10). They suggested that he insulted the Corinthians by refusing their financial support, and demeaned himself by continuing with his own craft (11:7-11). Moreover, they seem to have insinuated that Paul was soliciting money for the Jerusalem church under false pretenses (12:14-18).

Distracted From the True Meaning of the Gospel

According to Paul, these "false apostles" were simply out for their own benefit. In the process, they distracted the Corinthians from the true meaning of the gospel. Also in the process, they sought to discredit Paul, contending that he had not shown the usual "signs" of a true apostle (12:12).

Paul's response to this situation was especially pointed in 11:1-12:13. Quite reluctantly, he joined his rivals in self-boasting (see "An Outline of 2 Corinthians 10–13").

AN OUTLINE OF 2 CORINTHIANS 10–13

Warnings about false apostles	10:1–13:10
A call for obedience and understanding	10:1-18
A "fool's speech"	11:1–12:13
Prologue	11:1-21a
The speech proper	11:21b–12:10
Epilogue	12:11-13
Warnings in advance of a visit	12:14–13:10
Expressions of concern	12:14-21
Warning and admonition	13:1-10
Letter closing	13:11-13

Paul Recounted Dangers

Paul said that he had been forced to such foolishness because the Corinthians themselves had not come to his defense (12:11). The two main sections of this "fool's speech" read like parodies of his rivals' boasting. Paul parodied their recitals of heroic missionary achievements in 11:24-33, and their reports of extraordinary religious experiences in 12:1-10.

The statements that led up to these two parodies were more straightforward. We do not know why the false apostles had boasted about their Jewish heritage (11:22). Nonetheless, whatever they could claim in that regard, Paul could as well—quite legitimately. Further, if they were bold enough to present themselves as Christ's "ministers" (11:23), then Paul was bold enough to say that he is "a better one." Paul had been at greater risk—and more often—than they.

Paul sprang from his general reference about the dangers he had faced to the parody that follows in 11:24-33. In his day, rulers, military leaders, and other notables commonly compiled self-congratulatory accounts of their heroic exploits. The false apostles had probably done the same, listing their missionary accomplishments. This tact is not quite what we have from Paul, however. Paul listed only troubles—without providing specifics, except for the incident at Damascus. Moreover, he did not list these as evidence of his great faith, nor even of God's action in seeing him through adversities. Paul specifically said that he offered these accounts as evidence of his weakness (11:30).

Paul's reference to "all the churches" that he had founded (11:28-29) was part of the parody. Elsewhere he thought of his churches as attesting to his apostleship (3:1-5; 1 Corinthians 9:1-2). In this passage, however, he wanted to counteract the brazen claims of his rivals. Therefore, he mentioned "all the churches" only as further evidence of his weakness: he had to worry constantly that his work for the churches had not succeeded.

A Close Call in a Basket

The finest touch in this first parody comes right at the end. Paul recounted a close call that he once had in Damascus, probably shortly after his conversion. As the apostle told it, in order to avoid arrest he was forced to flee Damascus by hiding in a basket, which was then lowered through a window in the city wall (11:32-33; compare Acts 9:23-25).

The remainder of our passage (12:1-10) parodies the false apostles' boasting of their extraordinary religious experiences. "Well," Paul seems to be saying, "if it is tales of religious experiences that you want from your apostles, I'll tell you about two of my own." He described the first one (12:2-5) as if it were someone else's, but that seems to be part of the parody (note verse 5). With his remark that it happened "fourteen years ago," before even his first visit to Corinth, he was already making his point: although it was a highly unusual experience, he had never considered it important enough to tell them about.

As it turns out, there was very little to tell them about Paul's special religious episode. He experienced it as a journey to another realm ("the third heaven," or "Paradise"), but he had no notion of how he went. Moreover, he evidently saw nothing worth reporting. And although he heard "things," they were sounds that a mortal cannot repeat. Measured by other ancient accounts of such experiences, both Jewish and pagan, this one is distinctly second-rate!

Paul's first readers would have gotten the point at once. They knew that one of the highest honors the Roman emperor could bestow was a crown crafted of precious metal in the shape of a city wall. This rare award was bestowed on the first soldier to succeed in entering a city under siege by courageously scaling its wall. By contrast, Paul tells us, he was fleeing a city over its wall, and not to engage his adversaries but to escape engagement. He recounted this not as a heroic act, but as an act of cowardice, and therefore a further sign of his weakness.

A Thorn in the Flesh

After some further remarks about his reluctance to stoop to boasting, Paul mentioned a "thorn in the flesh" with which he was afflicted, attributing it to a "messenger of Satan" (12:7). This affliction might have been some chronic physical ailment, bothersome although certainly not disabling; but this reference does not present enough evidence for any theory. In any case, the important thing is how Paul interpreted the affliction, whatever it was: as a burden meant to keep him from being too elated about that long-ago religious experience.

The climax of this "fool's speech" is the apostle's report of how his prayers for removal of the "thorn" were finally answered.

The climax of this "fool's speech" is the apostle's report of how his prayers for removal of the "thorn" were finally answered (12:8-10). He was neither promised a miracle nor given instructions for finding relief on his own. Even pagans routinely expected either a miracle or divine instructions from their gods. What the Lord (the resurrected Christ) had answered Paul in response to his petitions was only, "My grace is sufficient for you, for power is made perfect in weakness" (12:9a).

Paul did not interpret this response to mean only that he was granted the patience to endure his weaknesses. Nor could his weaknesses somehow become "strengths." He understood it to mean that grace—"the power of Christ"—was present in and through his weaknesses (12:9b-10). This paradox is nothing else than the paradox of the gospel itself, as disclosed in the cross. Here, as elsewhere, Paul thought of his apostolic sufferings and weaknesses as part of his total proclamation of "the death of Jesus," and therefore of the life-giving power of the cross (2 Corinthians 4:10-12).

Dimension 3: What Does the Bible Mean to Us?

Distinguishing Marks of Christian Ministry

To many persons, the focus passage will not seem much like Scripture. It contains no specific affirmations of faith, religious instruction, or moral appeals. Moreover, it is confrontational, verging at points on sarcasm. Even so, beneath its sometimes overheated rhetoric, this passage responds to a question that is no less important for the church today than for the church in ancient Corinth: *What are the distinguishing marks of an authentically Christian ministry?* Here *ministry* will be used very broadly, to include the way Christian laypeople live out their faith in the world, the "representative ministry" of the church's clergy, and the ministries of the church as an institution in society.

Paul's rivals had their own ideas about authentic ministers and ministries. They required apostles to be of Jewish stock, willing to work hard and take risks, capable of heroically overcoming hardships, and self-evidently "religious." They probably also expected apostles to have the physical appearance and personal bearing that elicit instant respect.

Paul didn't make an issue about being Jewish, because he could match his rivals on that score (11:22). However, he certainly did not believe that sex, race, ethnic origin, or social position should ever disqualify one from ministry. For example, his trusted associate, Titus, was a Gentile (Galatians 2:3), and he held the female apostle, Junia, in highest regard (Romans 16:7).

Paul also rejected the notion that ministers must be "heroic" figures, able to overcome any adversity. He emphasized that they are as mortal and vulnerable as anyone else (2 Corinthians 4:7). Nor did he agree that displays of religious ecstasy either constitute or confirm a call to ministry; nor that physical appearance and personal bearing are necessary qualifications.

Four Marks of Authentic Ministry

In short, Paul put no stock in "image." He cared only that ministry have strong inner integrity. Four marks of such a ministry emerge in our passage:

1. The apostle agreed with his rivals that ministry requires plenty of hard work and a willingness to take risks (11:22; see also 1 Corinthians 15:10, 30-32). If hard work and a willingness to take risks are not present, one must doubt whether there is a deep enough understanding of the urgency of the task or commitment to it.

In Paul's own experience, ministry included the hard work of arduous travel and trying to make ends meet by continuing at his trade. In our day, ministry must be involved, especially, with the hard work of keeping the gospel alive and credible in a society that needs it more but heeds it less.

2. An authentically Christian ministry is especially concerned about the "weak." Although the evidence for this in our particular passage is indirect, it is unmistakable (11:28-29). Explaining his "anxiety for all the churches," the apostle posed two rhetorical questions: "Who is weak and I am not weak? Who is made to stumble, and I am not indignant?" (11:29)

The risks of ministry today are in large part the same as for Paul. They include the risks of unpopularity, loss of status, and even—in some places—incarceration or death for expressing views or taking actions that go against the grain of prevailing values and opinions. For us, as for Paul, there are sometimes risks within the church (from "false brothers and sisters," 11:26) as well as in "the world."

The first of these questions suggests that an authentically Christian ministry stands with the "weak," working on behalf of the gospel to deliver them from whatever prevents their flourishing in faith or as human beings. The second question suggests that an authentically Christian ministry does not hesitate to stand against whatever actions, policies, or structures are responsible for making and keeping people weak in their faith or as human beings. Who the "weak" are, and what the church's "standing with" and "standing against" must involve, will vary according to time and place. What does not change is the gospel's imperative to embrace the weak in love, as our brothers and sisters for whom Christ died (1 Corinthians 8:11).

3. For Paul, no ministry was authentically Christian that was not committed in principle and principally to preaching the word of the cross. This conviction led him to counter his rivals' boasting about worldly achievements with his own recital of woes and weaknesses. He interpreted these as showing Jesus' death (2 Corinthians 4:7-12), just as his preaching did. This explains his reference to what the Corinthians had "seen" in him and "heard" from him (12:6): in his weaknesses, as well as from his lips, they had been presented with the word of the cross.

We must not misunderstand. Paul was not encouraging suffering and weakness, as if these were Christian "virtues." He was only interpreting the afflictions and failures that he had already experienced as an apostle. They served to prevent making a hero of himself, and to disclose that the actual source and center of his ministry was the crucified Christ.

4. The critical test of an authentically Christian ministry is whether it seeks to make this word of the cross present in the world as a word of grace. For Paul, this single word, *grace*, summed up "the power of Christ" as he himself had experienced it (12:9). Through his ministry he sought to help others know that same saving presence of grace in their lives.

No less in our day than in Paul's, this remains the basic and legitimate task of all Christian ministry: *to give the grace of God, as we have experienced it in Christ, a meaningful presence in the world.*

Dimension 4:
A Daily Bible Journey Plan

Day 1: **2 Corinthians 11:1-15**

Day 2: **2 Corinthians 11:16-33**

Day 3: **2 Corinthians 12:1-21**

Day 4: **2 Corinthians 13:1-13**

Day 5: **Galatians 1:1-24**

Day 6: **Galatians 2:1-14**

Day 7: **Galatians 2:15–3:5**

11

CHILDREN OF PROMISE

What to Watch For

In this passage, Paul wrote about the liberating, life-changing reality that those persons who are in Christ experience. More particularly, he reminded his readers that their baptism into Christ unites them with one another as God's children and establishes them as heirs of the promise of life that was made to Abraham. As children of this promise, believers are set free from the various claims and fears that previously ruled their lives.

As he wrote of this new life, Paul drew a sharp, fundamental contrast between Christ and the law. Several other contrasts follow from this one:

➤ being under the law versus the life of faith;
➤ being a minor child versus being a full-fledged heir;
➤ being a slave versus being redeemed.

There are three key affirmations in this passage:
➤ the statements about the significance of baptism;
➤ God's sending of the Son (the Incarnation);
➤ God's sending of the Spirit.

Paul possibly echoed in each case affirmations of faith that were regularly used by his and other Christian congregations.

1. To what three things were the Galatians enslaved before they became Christians?

2. What did Paul specify as the purpose of redemption?

3. What two things happen in baptism?

4. What special concern did Paul have about the Galatians?

To the Churches of Galatia

In Galatians, Paul addressed not just one congregation but several. Moreover, he was deeply worried about them. He feared that the members of these congregations were on the verge of "deserting" the gospel he had proclaimed to them by embracing another interpretation of the gospel—a teaching that he refused to call a "gospel" at all (1:6-9).

We cannot recover the exact origins and content of the false teaching. Note, however, one important, clear point about the false teaching: It sought to teach the Galatian Christians that Gentile converts must bind themselves to some of the requirements of the Jewish law if they hoped to receive the Spirit.

Because most, if not all, of the Galatian Christians were Gentiles, this false teaching affected them directly. In particular, they were urged to adhere to the laws about circumcision (see 5:2-3; 6:12-15); clean and unclean foods (see 2:11-14); and observing certain special days, seasons, and years (see 4:9-10). In Paul's view, however, none of these requirements should have been imposed on Gentiles. He labeled them "works of the law," and argued that the Galatians had already received God's Spirit when they responded in faith to his preaching of Jesus Christ crucified (3:1-5).

You will find evidence of the depth of Paul's concern about this matter throughout the letter. Right at the beginning, he substituted a general warning for his usual complimentary paragraph of thanksgiving; and then at the end, he highlighted his concern with an earnest summary paragraph (see "An Outline of Galatians").

AN OUTLINE OF GALATIANS

Letter opening	1:1-5
General warning	1:6-10
Paul's call to apostleship	1:11-24
The truth of the gospel	2:1-21
Tested in Jerusalem	2:1-10
Defended in Antioch	2:11-21
Demonstrations of the gospel's truth	3:1–5:12
The gospel and the Galatians	3:1-5
The gospel and Abraham	3:6-18
The gospel and the law	3:19–5:12
General appeals	5:13–6:10
Fulfill the law through love	5:13-15
Live by the Spirit	5:16-23
Fulfill the law of Christ	6:1-10
Summary and letter closing	6:11-18.

Life Under the Law

Our focus passage stands in a section where the apostle was especially intent on showing the difference between life under the law and life according to the gospel. The reference to Abraham in 3:6-18 helps him do this. As in Romans (chapter 4), he pointed out that even this revered patriarch of Israel had lived by faith—relying not on the law, but only on God's promise.

Then why was the law given at all? Paul himself posed this question (3:19a). He began at once to sketch out an answer to it (3:19b-22). His comments are not easy to follow and are, therefore, open to various interpretations. However, at least three points are clear:

- The law, even though it does not contradict God's promises, plays only a secondary and temporary role in God's plan.
- The law remains utterly powerless to give life.
- Only God's promise—as faith receives it through Jesus Christ—is able to free humankind from its bondage to sin.

The temporary status of the law was still in view in 3:23-24. Before "Christ came"—which meant, also, "before faith came"—the law served as "disciplinarian." Paul seems to be saying that the law's role was to point sin out, thereby bringing it to "Life" in the universal human experience of guilt (Romans 7:7-11). By thus "multiplying" and enlarging sin's presence (see Romans 5:20), the law was preparing for Christ's saving work. As Paul saw it, however, the Law itself remained sin's hostage, had only a preliminary function, and was without any power to save.

Life Under the Gospel

In Paul's day, the word that was translated in the NRSV as "disciplinarian" was used to describe any household slave to whom responsibility had been assigned for supervising the minor children. This family imagery is continued in Galatians 3:25-29. "But now that faith has come," the apostle said, "we are no longer subject to a disciplinarian" (the law) as minor children; rather, "in Christ Jesus" we are fully the children of God. To nail down his point, Paul reminded his readers about their baptism, calling it a baptism "into Christ." Changing the metaphor, he portrayed it as "clothing" oneself with Christ. He meant that in baptism Christians are taking on a completely new life, a new identity.

This new identity that comes with baptism also involves incorporation into a new family. Paul's striking phrase, "baptized into Christ" already hints at this identity; Christian baptism is always "into" a community of believers. The oneness of this family of faith derives from the relationship that each of its members has with Christ. In "the world," people are identified mainly with reference to their race, ethnic origin, cultural heritage, gender, and social status; but in Christ, these identifications seem to be only incidental to who we are, not decisive. In stating this idea, Paul may well have been quoting from a baptismal liturgy in common use: "There is no longer Jew or Greek, there is no longer slave or free, there is no longer male and female; for all of you are one in Christ Jesus" (3:28). Racial, ethnic, cultural, gender, and social differences remain, of course, but no longer in a way that alienates people from one another. In Christ, this diversity is embraced and affirmed, to the enrichment of the whole community.

Made One of Abraham's Offspring

When Paul added that baptism also makes one "Abraham's offspring" (3:29), he wanted the Gentile Christians of Galatia to pay strict attention. Because Christ, not the law, is the "offspring" to whom God's promises were made through Abraham (3:16-18), Gentiles who have been baptized into Christ have already become "heirs according to the promise" (29). It is not true, as the false teaching claims, that Gentiles must adopt certain Jewish practices in order to be Christians.

In 4:1-7, Paul combined his description of Christians as "heirs" of God's promise to Abraham with his image of the law as a "disciplinarian." Like minor children who have no more right to the family inheritance than the household slave by whom they are disciplined, people who rely on God's law instead of God's promise are not truly heirs. Although Paul did not think of the law as evil, he believed that those who look to it for life are in fact "enslaved to the elemental spirits of the world" (4:3). Like the affirmations in 3:25-29, those in 4:4-7 offer descriptions of the new life in Christ. As before the apostle made use of some statements of faith that had already attained the status of Christian traditions.

> Paul probably had in mind unseen demonic forces, the unnamed "beings that by nature are not gods" (4:8-9) to which he, like most people in the ancient world, attributed the evils that were otherwise hard to explain.

One of these (4:4-5) affirms that "God sent his Son" to free humankind from the law (and therefore, from sin). Three points are of special interest. First, by describing the Son as "born of a woman," the statement calls attention to his humanity; being God's Son did not make him less human. However, nothing is said or implied about how he was conceived, or of what woman he was born. If Paul knew any traditions about a "virgin birth," or about Mary and Joseph, that is not evident here (or anywhere else in his letters).

Second, by describing God's Son as "born under the law," it called attention to his Jewishness. More important, it suggests that he was able to identify with the situation of all those who are under the law's control.

Third, nothing is said about how the Son's redemptive mission is fulfilled. Our attention is directed only to the reality of being freed from the law and "adopted" as God's children; with this, we have become "heirs" of the promise in the fullest sense (4:7).

Abba! Father!

Further traditional formulas are echoed in the statement about God's having "sent the Spirit of his Son into our hearts, crying, 'Abba! Father!'" (4:6). Paul himself made no distinction between "the Spirit of God" and

The specific cry, "Abba! Father!" could derive from early Christian baptismal ceremonies, where it may have been uttered by the newly baptized as an expression of their new relationship to God (compare Romans 8:14-16).

"the Spirit of Christ" (see Romans 8:9-11), and none is implied in this statement, either. The word *abba* is Aramaic, which was the language spoken by Jews and Jewish-Christians in first-century Palestine. "Abba" was such a traditional way of addressing God, that it seems to have been retained even by Greek-speaking Christians, along with the Greek word for "Father." In everyday Aramaic, *abba* was the affectionate term by which children addressed their fathers. When used in addressing God, it expresses the believers' sense of their closeness to the heavenly "Father."

It was their new relationship to God, celebrated at their baptism, that Paul wanted the Galatian Christians to remember. If they now subjected themselves to the law, as some false teachers wanted them to do, they would abandon the promise through which their lives had been made new. Paul was worried that exactly this might happen (4:8-11).

Dimension 3:
What Does the Bible Mean to Us?

The Journey From Law to Life

It may appear on the face of it that Paul's warnings to the Galatians about the law have no meaning at all for us. The false teaching that he criticized has long since disappeared, and would be almost impossible to revive in our modern world. Few present-day Christians could be persuaded that it is necessary to adopt Jewish practices, like circumcision and kosher dining to be a real Christian. However, as Paul himself knew, there are also other ways of living "under the law" which compromise, no less seriously, "the truth of the gospel."

For example, we are living "under the law" if we suppose that being a Christian means, basically, doing certain things and not doing certain other things. How many times have we heard, or said, "Christians don't do that," or "Christians ought to do this"? There are, of course, certain actions that most Christians would condemn, and other actions that most Christians would commend. The problem comes if we begin thinking of these dos and don'ts as absolutes, and identifying them with the gospel itself.

This is a problem, first, because the gospel is fundamentally about what *God* has done, not about what we "ought to do." It is the "good news" of God's affirming and saving grace.

Thinking of the gospel as a set of dos and don'ts is a problem, second, because God's claim on our lives cannot be reduced to mere rules or to so-called "Christian standards." When Paul, for instance, referred to "the law of Christ" in Galatians 6:2, he did not mean that Jesus replaced the laws of the Old Testament with new "Christian rules." He meant that in Christ we have been claimed by a love that asks far more than any set of rules could ever ask (see 5:13-14). Specific laws and rules can be formally "obeyed," but God's claim to be a loving person is like a debt that can never be repaid (see Romans 13:8-10). Faith accepts the boundless gift of God's love as a boundless call to love.

We are also living "under the law" if we suppose that being a Christian means, basically, accepting one specific set of "beliefs" as true beyond question. For example, we often hear something like, "If you believe that God (or Christ) did so and so (or is able to do so and so), then you will be saved." Again, there are two problems with this.

Every statement about God remains simply a human statement about God. Even though some are undoubtedly truer to the Christian experience of God than others, none can claim to be "the gospel truth." The gospel can never be reduced to a creed or other theological summary, no matter how elegantly formulated it may be.

Statements about faith are important and useful. However, if we turn them into objects of faith, we are deserting the gospel itself in order to live "under the law."

What this passage suggests about the significance of Christian baptism also merits our attention. Three points are important.

> The gospel is fundamentally about what God has done, not about what we "ought to do."

A Rite of Passage?

For Christians, baptism is a "rite of passage." It identifies the baptized person as one who has been "clothed" with Christ and is now embarked on a new way of life. Many people think of baptism as the occasion when a person's given name ("Susan," "John," and so forth) is "officially" bestowed. But in fact, the most important name that is bestowed at baptism is Christ's: the one baptized is now recognized and celebrated as "Christ-ian."

We do not know whether Paul or other first-century Christians practiced infant baptism. Perhaps, like some Christians today, they baptized only persons mature enough to commit themselves to the new life that this new identity involves. Or perhaps, like other Christians today, they celebrated baptism primarily as God's affirming and claiming of a person's life.

Neither of these practices can be excluded on the basis of the New Testament.

This rite of passage is into a community of baptized persons. The new identity of each is actualized in relation to all of the others. On this point, the New Testament leaves us in no doubt. Christian baptism is not to be a private affair. It is a community rite. Those who are now given Christ's name are at the same time established within a new family. They have become one with all others who bear the name of Christ.

> Faith expresses itself not as mere statements about what we are willing to "believe," but in the way we actually live our lives.

Moreover, baptism initiates us into a family of faith that is called not simply to tolerate but to celebrate diversity. In Christ we are to affirm one another in our racial, ethnic, sexual, cultural, and social individuality. This celebration of diversity is integral, not just incidental, to life in the household of faith, because it bears witness to God's own impartiality.

Finally, those who have been baptized into Christ are called to live henceforth as "heirs according to the promise." This means life in Christ, as distinguished from life under the law. More specifically, as Paul had indicated later on in Galatians, living as children of promise means to be agents of God's love (5:13-15); to be guided and empowered by God's Spirit (5:16-23); and to fulfill the law of Christ (6:1-10).

Dimension 4: A Daily Bible Journey Plan

Day 1: **Galatians 3:6-22**

Day 2: **Galatians 3:23–4:11**

Day 3: **Galatians 4:12–5:1**

Day 4: **Galatians 5:2-15**

Day 5: **Galatians 5:16-26**

Day 6: **Galatians 6:1-18**

Day 7: **Ephesians 1:1-23**

Ephesians 2:1-22

12

ONE NEW HUMANITY

What to Watch For

The focus passage is typical of Ephesians as a whole. Here, as elsewhere, the author wanted his Gentile Christian readers to know that, with their conversion to the gospel, they had become one with God's people, "the commonwealth of Israel" (Ephesians 2:12). In Christ, the old wall between Gentiles and Jews had been broken down (2:14). In him, these two groups had been constituted as "one new humanity" and, together, reconciled to God (2:15-16).

As this major point was developed, several other themes emerged:

➤ Gentiles had been destined from eternity to be saved from their sins and included within the people of God.
➤ The Gentiles' new life as believers was radically different from their past life as pagans. They had been raised with Christ and seated with him in heaven.
➤ The Gentiles' salvation had been accomplished by God's grace, through faith, and by means of Christ's death and resurrection.
➤ The Gentiles experienced this new resurrection life within the church, which manifested the one new humanity that had been given in Christ.

93

1. According to this passage, why did God create human beings?

2. What two groups were once divided by a wall of hostility?

3. In what two ways is Christ identified with "peace"?

4. Who forms the "foundation" for God's household, who is its "corner-stone," and what does it "grow into"?

Dimension 2:
What Does the Bible Mean?

Although Ephesians was probably not written by Paul (see "The Special Character of Ephesians" in the box on page 95), the author was an important representative of Paul's thought as it was taken up by others in the decades after the apostle's death.

However, this writer did not merely reproduce Paul's thinking. He tapped into it, adapted it, and developed it in order to address matters that especially concerned him.

Most of all, the author wanted to lead his readers into a deeper understanding of what he called "the mystery of Christ" (3:4). One aspect of this "mystery" was Christ's role as "head" of the church (for example, 1:22). Another was the inclusion of uncircumcised Gentiles as "fellow heirs" of God's promise with the Jews (3:6). Our focus passage is a major part of the section within which this "mystery of Christ" is being unfolded (see "An Outline of Ephesians," page 97).

THE SPECIAL CHARACTER OF EPHESIANS

Ephesians has several features that set it apart from the Pauline letters.

- First, it reads more like an essay intended for Christians in many places besides Ephesus than like a pastoral letter sent to a specific congregation or group of congregations. This corresponds with the fact that, originally, the name *Ephesus* seems not to have stood in the letter's address (see the NRSV footnote to Ephesians 1:1).

- Second, there are a number of close parallels between the contents of Ephesians and Colossians. In some instances, the actual wording is the same.

- Third, many of the ideas expressed in Ephesians do not represent Paul's thinking in his letters to the Romans, Corinthians, Galatians, Philippians, and Thessalonians.

- Fourth, the literary style and some of the terminology of Ephesians are also not typically that which scholars recognize as being from Paul.

Generally, but not unanimously, scholars have concluded that Ephesians was written by someone other than Paul himself, perhaps twenty to thirty years after the apostle's death. We can understand why this unknown author would have chosen to distribute his own work as Paul's. He had been deeply influenced by Paul's thought, and might even have known him personally. It was not uncommon, in the ancient world, for followers of important teachers to use the master's name on their own writings. This both identified the tradition in which their writing stood, and helped it to be noticed and taken seriously.

Most scholars have concluded that the author of Ephesians made special use of Colossians as he wrote. However, a comparison of the two writings shows that the author also did not hesitate to alter the materials that he took over from Colossians. By observing these changes, and also the passages that are unique to Ephesians, we can better appreciate this writer's special interests and point of view.

However, this writer did not merely reproduce Paul's thinking. He tapped into it, adapted it, and developed it in order to address matters that especially concerned him.

Most of all, the author wanted to lead his readers into a deeper understanding of what he called "the mystery of Christ" (3:4). One aspect of this "mystery" was Christ's role as "head" of the church (for example, 1:22). Another was the inclusion of uncircumcised Gentiles as "fellow heirs" of God's promise with the Jews (3:6). Our focus passage is a major part of the section within which this "mystery of Christ" is being unfolded (see "An Outline of Ephesians").

The first paragraph, 2:1-10, is about resurrection with Christ. The second, 2:11-22, is about reconciliation in Christ.

The affirmation at the heart of 2:1-10 comes in verses 4-6. God, acting with love and mercy, "made us alive together with Christ . . . and raised us up with him and seated us with him in the heavenly places. . . ."

Saved From the Wrath We Deserve

The whole of humanity was deserving of God's wrath. However, humanity had been saved from the wrath it deserved. Echoing Paul's own magnificent statements about God's unconditional love and saving grace (see especially, Romans 5:6, 8), the writer emphasized that salvation "is the gift of God—not the result of works" (8-9). In fact, as his next comment showed, he understood "good works" to be the result of salvation! He believed that it was God's plan, even before creation, to create humanity anew in Christ for good works (10).

In verses 11-12, for the second time in this passage, the writer reminded his readers about their pre-Christian life. The first time he had written about their past immorality (1-3). Now he reminded them that, as Gentile unbelievers, they had also been alienated from "the covenants of promise" that God had made with Israel. Therefore, they had been alienated from God as well, and were without hope.

A Key Affirmation

The key affirmation in this second paragraph of the passage is the statement in verse 13, "But now in Christ Jesus," by his death (see also "through the cross," 16), the Gentiles who were once "far off" have been "brought near." The author had two things in mind, and they were inseparable. Above all, Christ's death had brought the

Gentiles near to God (see 16 and 18). At the same time, they had been brought near to "the commonwealth of Israel" (12), God's covenant people (14-17). Just how inseparable these two were is evident from verses 14-18, where the writer's comments shifted back and forth from one to the other.

Three powerful images were employed to express what had been accomplished through Christ's death:

"The dividing wall" between Jews and Gentiles had been broken down (14). This was a reference to the law, which the Jews had understood to be their special possession and the basis of their unique status as the people of God. But now Christ had abolished the law (15a), and with this the age-old barrier between the Gentiles and the covenant people had been removed.

Christ had become our "peace" (14). Not only had the dividing wall of hostility been torn down; one could also speak of reconciliation.

Christ's work was to "create in himself one new humanity" (15b). The writer might have been building on Romans 5:12-21, where Paul had portrayed Christ as the second "Adam," a name formed from the Hebrew word, *humanity*. Now, in Christ, humanity was no longer divided into two groups—"God's people" (Jews), and all the rest (Gentiles). Now the two had been re-created as "one body" (16). Moreover, as one new humanity they had access to God "in one Spirit" (18).

Our passage concludes with a portrayal of the church as the place where this one new humanity was already visible (19-22). The image of the church as God's "household" (19) was combined initially with an image of the church as a building (20), and then, more specifically, with

AN OUTLINE OF EPHESIANS

Letter opening	1:1-2
Blessing	1:3-14
Thanksgiving	1:15-23
Affirmations about the mystery of Christ	2:1–3:21
Resurrection and reconciliation	2:1-22
Paul's stewardship of God's grace	3:1-13
Prayer and doxology	3:14-21
Appeals	4:1–6:20
For unity	4:1-16
To lead a new life	4:17–5:20
Concerning life in the household	5:21-6:9
To be strong in the Lord and pray in the Spirit	6:10-20
Letter closing	6:21-24

an image of the church as "a holy temple in the Lord" (21-22). All three
of these images were present in Paul's own letters (God's "household,"
Galatians 6:10; a building under construction, 1 Corinthians 3:9-11;
God's "temple," 1 Corinthians 3:16-17). However, the writer had gone
beyond Paul's imagery in two respects.

He combined them in a way that Paul never did. The result was a
strikingly dynamic concept of the church as a living structure. Its foundation was constituted by the apostles and prophets, its "keystone" (see
NRSV footnote to verse 20) was Christ Jesus, and believers were "built
together spiritually" into it.

His portrayal of the church as founded on the apostles and Christian
(not Hebrew) prophets was a departure from Paul's imagery in
1 Corinthians 3:9-11. Paul identified Christ as the foundation, himself as
the master builder who put it into place (in Corinth and elsewhere), and
other ministers as workers who built upon it. However, this writer, look-
ing back two or three decades, accorded the apostles a higher status. To
him, they were the guarantors of the gospel, "holy apostles" (3:5), and
therefore foundational for the church's life.

Having represented the apostles and Christian prophets as the
church's foundation, the writer was left with the problem of portraying
Christ in some yet higher role. His solution was to describe Christ as the
building's "keystone," which was a stone placed at the very crown of an
arch to bind the whole structure together. This image was an especially
appropriate one, since it corresponded to the writer's conception of
Christ as the "head" of the church (4:15; 5:23).

Dimension 3:
What Does the Bible Mean to Us?

The Importance of Ephesians
Some may question whether Ephesians can have any significance for us
today if, in fact, it was written years after Paul's death by a person who
only used the apostle's name. Does this make Ephesians less important
than the letters we know to be Paul's own (Romans, First and Second
Corinthians, Galatians, Philippians, First Thessalonians, and Philemon)?

Absolutely not. Ephesians remains a very important and guiding docu-
ment. In this connection, three points are worth bearing in mind:
● The author had no intent whatever to deceive his readers. As noted in
Dimension 2, he was identifying the tradition in which he himself sought
to stand.
● No matter who the author was, Ephesians remains an honored part of
Christian Scripture. For almost two thousand years this letter has been

read and appreciated by the church. It has stood the test of time and can still be a guiding document for us. To the extent that this author's thought modified or went beyond Paul's own, we are the richer for having another voice in the scriptural chorus of faith.

• Just as we can better appreciate Paul's own letters when we understand their respective historical settings, so can we better appreciate Ephesians when we are aware of its particular historical setting. Simply "pretending" that it is Paul's, although it is not, deprives us of what this writer had to say. Indeed, we honor the scriptural status of Ephesians most when we read it on its own terms. Our task is to discover what is most distinctive about this later writer's thought, and consider what it can mean for us.

One New Humanity

A particularly distinctive aspect of our focus passage is the emphasis on Christ as representative of "one new humanity"—a bold and provocative affirmation, even today.

It offers a vision of God's love and purpose as embracing even those who do not specifically profess faith in Christ. To be sure, the writer presented Christ as defining who God is and what humanity's relationship to God is. However, he had not presented Christ as some new "wall" for separating "believers" from "nonbelievers." In that case, Christ would simply be a barrier like the law that he had abolished! Rather, the Letter to the Ephesians affirmed Christ as representative of a love that embraces the whole of humanity.

A Remarkable Vision

What might this remarkable vision suggest, for example, about the church's commission to "go and make disciples of all nations"? (The church's preaching to nonbelievers should not be done arrogantly or self-righteously.) If we accept this writer's view of the one new humanity that is already created in Christ, then the message will not be proclaimed as a threat; for example, "Accept Christ, or else!" Rather, the church's message really will be the gospel—that is, "the good news," and therefore an invitation: "In Christ, you are already God's people, and we invite you to celebrate and demonstrate this reality, along with us, in the community of faith."

A Decisive Question

This vision, nevertheless, does not mean that whatever people think about their life, or however they live it out, can be affirmed as true and right. Nor does it mean that all religious beliefs and practices are equally true and right. It is not the church's place to condemn other religions outright, but to seek dialogue with them, and mutual understanding. Because this is love's way, it is also the best way to bear witness to Christ.

The writer certainly did not downplay the importance of the church. He strongly affirmed it, as the community where the one new humanity was most visibly and specifically present in the world.

He portrayed it, initially, as the "household" (19) of the heavenly "Father" to whom we all have access "in the one Spirit" (18). In the church, we are to affirm and cherish one another as spiritual sisters and brothers. However, this household is much more than just a wholesome place to enjoy one another's company, or just a "support group" to help people pursue their individual "spiritual journeys." These functions, however important, are incidental to what the church is all about.

Two further, closely related metaphors speak more directly to the purpose of the church. By portraying it as "a holy temple" and "the dwelling place for God" (21-22), our author suggested that it exists, fundamentally, for the praise of God. His more general description of it as a building founded on the apostles and prophets, with Christ as the keystone (20), was equally important. This temple's "architecture," that which properly shaped and informed both its worship and its work, was the apostolic witness to Jesus Christ. What this witness is and means are matters to which the church is called to give its careful, close, and continuing attention.

Dimension 4:
A Daily Bible Journey Plan

Day 1: **Ephesians 2:1-22**

Day 2: **Ephesians 3:1-21**

Day 3: **Ephesians 4:1-16**

Day 4: **Ephesians 4:17–5:2**

Day 5: **Ephesians 5:3-20**

Day 6: **Ephesians 5:21–6:9**

Day 7: **Ephesians 6:10-24**

ONE NAME ABOVE ALL

What to Watch For

Read Philippians 1:27–2:13.This passage comes from a section of appeals that extends from 1:27 through 2:18. For the most part, these were general appeals to live a Christian life. Being Christian in Philippi, however, had been made somewhat difficult because of certain unnamed "opponents" (1:28).

As he proceeded with and supported these appeals, Paul made use of an elegant hymn in praise of Christ (2:6-11). This hymn seems to have two main parts, each of which can be divided into three smaller units.

➤ The first part describes Christ's action in "emptying" himself and becoming "obedient to the point of death" (6-8).
➤ The second part describes God's action in exalting Christ and making him "Lord" (verses 9-11).

One may read this passage as a whole, noting how Paul had used the Christ hymn in the context of this letter. Focusing on just the hymn is equally rewarding, imagining how it might have functioned in the context of an early Christian church assembled for worship.

1. What two privileges had God granted the Philippians?

2. What could the Philippians do to fulfill Paul's joy?

3. Whose actions were described in verses 6-8 and what were they?

4. Whose actions were described in verses 9-11, and what were they?

Philippians was written while Paul was in prison. The apostle seemed hopeful of eventual release, however, and anticipated returning to Philippi (1:25-26). Meanwhile, he was concerned that the Philippian Christians remain steadfast and united in their faith. The appeals in 1:27–2:18 reflect this concern (see "An Outline of Philippians").

AN OUTLINE OF PHILIPPIANS

Letter opening	1:1-2
Thanksgiving	1:3-11
Report about Paul's present circumstances	1:12-26
Appeals to live in a manner worthy of the gospel	1:27–2:18
A hymn to Christ	2:6-11
Reports about Timothy and Epaphroditus	2:19–3.1a
Warnings and further appeals	3:1b–4:9
Warnings about unnamed opponents	3:1b-4a
Warnings supported	3:4b-16
Various appeals	3:17–4:9
Expressions of gratitude	4:10-20
Letter closing	4:21-23.

A Concern for Unity

The opening appeals (1:27-30) of this letter indicate that Paul's congregation was under some kind of pressure by people he identified only as "opponents" (1:28). Whoever they were, Paul regarded them as a threat both to the faith of the congregation and to its unity.

The apostle's concern for the congregation's unity was especially evident in 2:1-4. In urging his readers to be united in their faith, he appealed initially to their experience of the love they had known "in Christ," and as they had been partners "in the Spirit" (1). He also appealed to their present concern about his own situation (2). (What joy it would bring him to learn that there was "full accord" in their congregation!) Perhaps he was thinking specifically of the disagreement between Eudoia and Syntyche, two leading women in the congregation (4:2-3). In any case, Paul offered a special rule of thumb for Christian community: one should put the interests of others ahead of one's own (3-4; compare 1 Corinthians 10:24, 32-33). This, he believed, was love's way (1 Corinthians 13:5), because it was the way that had been disclosed in Christ's ultimate giving of himself for the sake of others (Romans 15:2-3).

To support his appeals, Paul quoted a hymn that praised Christ by describing his saving work (Philippians 2:6-11). No one knows when, where, or by whom this hymn was composed. Was it used only among Paul's congregations, or also beyond them? Was it "chanted" or "sung," and by whom? Questions such as these simply have to remain open. Nonetheless, most scholars today acknowledge the hymnic character of these verses, and the likelihood that this hymn was actually used by some first century congregations. (See "Early Christian Hymns," on page 104).

A Hymn of Praise

We need first to consider the hymn in itself, without reference to the way Paul used it in this letter. It was a hymn in praise of Christ as Lord. This praise was offered in the form of a story. The story was not about Jesus' earthly life, however. This hymn portrayed the awesome, cosmic drama of Christ's giving up "equality with God," taking human form, and then being exalted as "Lord."

The first part of the hymn (6-8) narrated Christ's action. It focused on his relinquishing heavenly status, descending into human history, humbling himself, and becoming "obedient even to the point of death." The Greek phrase translated as "born in human likeness" did not mean that Christ only seemed to be human; it affirmed the full reality of his humanity.

How, exactly, are we to interpret the references to Christ's humbling himself and becoming obedient? There is no doubt that these words appropriately describe Jesus' life and ministry as we know about them from the Gospels. However, in the context of this hymn, the one climactic event in

EARLY CHRISTIAN HYMNS

Apart from the heavenly visions in the Book of Revelation, there are only two places in the New Testament where singing is portrayed. One is in the account of Jesus' last supper with his disciples, where they sang "the hymn" before going out to the Mount of Olives (Mark 14:26; Matthew 26:30). The other is in the account of Paul's imprisonment in Philippi, where he and Silas are said to have been singing hymns in the middle of the night (Acts 16:25). Perhaps Jesus and his disciples used one of the psalms traditionally sung by the Jews at Passover. We have no idea what Paul and Silas might have been singing.

Some hymnlike passages in the New Testament later became Christian hymns and remain in use today. The most notable of these are the canticles that we know as the Magnificat (Luke 1:46-55), the Benedictus (Luke 1:68-72), and the Nunc Dimittis (Luke 2:29-32). However, these psalm-like materials probably did not originate as hymns. Similarly, the hymns in the Book of Revelation (for example, 5:9-10; 15:3-4) seem to have been composed specifically for that context. They were not drawn from the actual worship services of the church.

However, the New Testament does yield traces of hymns that may actually have been used in Christian worship. The two most outstanding and probable examples are Philippians 2:6-11 and Colossians 1:15-20. In each case, the hymn is about Christ; and in each case, it had been adapted in certain respects to fit the context of the letter in which it had been quoted.

view was Jesus' death. In obedience to God, Christ identified himself with the human condition even to the extent of becoming mortal, subjecting himself to death.

The extra phrase, "even death on a cross," breaks the hymnic pattern, and is so typically Pauline that many interpreters believe Paul himself added it.

The second part of the hymn (verses 9-11) narrated God's action. Christ's descent from heaven into death was not the end of the drama, only its beginning. Now the direction was reversed, from earth to heaven. Now the hymn sang of how God exalted Jesus and bestowed on him "the name that is above every name."

Several special points are worth noting:
- There is no mention of Jesus' resurrection, only of his exaltation.
- We are told that Christ was "highly exalted" (literally, super-exalted) by God.

He was not simply restored to his former status, but accorded a new status.

- The name that has been bestowed on Jesus is "Lord." This designates what his super-exalted status is.

Jesus Christ Is Lord

The final subsections of the hymn emphasized Christ's super-exalted status. He was the ruler of the whole cosmos, and as such was due universal praise (the specifying of "heaven," "earth," and "under the earth" reflected the ancient belief in a three-tiered universe). Wherever Christ's rule was recognized, people would join together in the words of the church's creed (perhaps its very earliest): "Jesus Christ is Lord." However, these words did not mean that Christ had replaced God. Because Christ had been exalted by God's action, to praise Christ as Lord was to give glory to God.

Why had Paul quoted this hymn of praise in the middle of his appeals for unity and steadfastness? What was there about it that struck him as appropriate for the present context? Two rather different answers have been proposed.

One possibility is that Paul quoted the hymn in order to hold up Christ as an example for the Philippians to follow. Just as he humbled himself and was willing to risk even death in order to be obedient to God, so should they. The mention of Christ's humility would fit in with the appeals to be concerned about the interests of others (verses 3-4); and the mention of Christ's obedience would fit in with Paul's hope that the Philippians would continue to obey his own counsels (12). This is the interpretation represented by the main NRSV translation of verse 5, where Paul introduced the hymn: the Philippians were to have the same mind "that was in Christ Jesus."

Another possible translation has Paul referring to the mind "that you have in Christ Jesus" (NRSV footnote to verse 5). If this is correct, Paul quoted the hymn in order to remind his readers of who they were as a community that acknowledged Christ as Lord. The "mind" that should guide them in relating to one another and in withstanding their opponents was the mind they had as they acknowledged Christ to be their Lord, to the glory of God.

> In confessing Christ as Lord, the Philippians were affirming the glory of God, and God's gracious, saving presence in their midst.

This second interpretation is the more likely. For one thing, it corresponds to what the hymn itself was all about. Neither Paul nor the hymn conceived of Christ simply as a "model" for faith. Because Christ was "Lord," he was the ground and object of faith. It also corresponds more closely to Paul's follow-up appeal in verses 12-13, which was not really about obedience. The Philippians were summoned to "work out [their] own salvation" in the confidence that God was already at work among them.

Remain Steadfast and United

Paul's summons to the Philippian Christians to remain steadfast and united
in their faith can be readily applied to the church in any age and place. In
this general sense, our passage has a clear and present meaning for us.
Like the believers in ancient Philippi, Christians today are also sometimes
tempted to slacken in their faith because of opposition. Sometimes our
faith is threatened by opposition from hostile governments, organizations,
religions, or cultural trends. But perhaps at least as often, the threat comes
from within the church itself, as apparently it did in Philippi.

As we consider how, more specifically, this passage can have meaning
for us, we must be careful not to misunderstand several of Paul's remarks
to the Philippians. Four of these, in particular, may be identified.

Suffering for Christ

Paul commented that God's grace had granted the Philippians the privilege
of suffering for Christ as well as believing in him (1:29).
We should note, first, that the apostle was referring only to suffering for
Christ—suffering which is brought on because of our commitment to the
gospel. He did not mean that all suffering is a privilege. Second, he did not
say that suffering is something we should seek, as though it could make us
"better Christians." Suffering for Christ is God's doing, a gift. Third, he
did not mean that we should deny the fact of suffering when we experience it, or be indifferent to the suffering of others. He meant that where
suffering for Christ can be neither avoided nor relieved, we are nonetheless able to cope with it by viewing it as part of our witness to the gospel.

In short, we are not asked to "accept" suffering by simply surrendering
to its inevitability. We are reminded that, whatever faith's present trials
and hardships, God always has "the last word," and that God's purposes
will prevail.

Be of One Mind

Several times in this passage, the apostle's call for unity was expressed as
a concern that the church be of "one mind" (1:27; 2:2, 5—although the
Greek expressions vary). Being of one mind does not mean that all
Christians are supposed to believe exactly the same—for example, about
God, Jesus, the Bible, or heaven and hell. Nor does it mean that all
Christians are supposed to hold exactly the same opinions about the moral
and ethical requirements of the gospel. In both respects, the apostle him-
self allowed for diversity within his congregations.

The church is not called to either uniformity of belief or practice, but unity in the Spirit. To be of "one mind" means to be united in accepting the boundless grace and claim of God as revealed in Jesus Christ. It also means to be united in our commitment to the ongoing task of living out God's grace in the world.

A Call to Humility

We must also be careful not to misinterpret Paul's instruction to "regard others as better than yourselves" (2:3). If taken out of context, this statement could be a very destructive word to people who already lack a healthy sense of self-worth. Read in context, Paul's counsel is a call to Christian humility (2:3) and attentiveness to the interests of others, not (just) to one's own interests (2:4).

To look out for the interests of others means to be respectful of their commitments, needs, and views, whether we are able to share them or not. Respect for the interests of others must sometimes be expressed as an invitation to engage in dialogue about the validity of what they perceive to be their "interests." This is where the "humility" comes in. There can be no honest and constructive dialogue without an openness to learn and have one's own views corrected.

The counsel not to look out for one's own interests doesn't mean being heedless of one's own physical, material, or spiritual needs. The gospel's summons to serve others presupposes that our own basic needs are being met. Paul's counsel means that we are not to pursue our own interests or fulfill our own needs at the expense of others. It means that we are not to take advantage of others in order to achieve our own goals.

God's Gift of Salvation

The counsel to "work out your own salvation" (2:12) is also misunderstood if it is taken out of context. The apostle did not mean that people have to achieve salvation on their own. He insisted repeatedly, throughout his letters, that salvation is God's gift. Indeed, the presupposition of the call to "work out [our] own salvation" is that God is already at work among us, making it possible for us "both to will and to work for his good pleasure" (2:13).

Be Agents of God's Grace

Our attention to the appeals in this passage ought not distract us from the hymn that Paul quoted in order to support them (2:6-11). This message is the centerpiece of the passage, and perhaps of the whole letter.

Above all, we must appreciate that this is a hymn. It was written and first used as an act of congregational praise. If we try to dissect it theologically, point by point, we will end up missing the whole point! It was never intended as a statement of doctrine, a summary of what we believe about Christ. It was meant as a vehicle for the believing community to celebrate its life in Christ. It is a way of identifying ourselves with the whole universe in praising Jesus Christ as Lord, "to the glory of God the Father."

This congregational hymn is an apt reminder that faith can never be a "solo performance." Although the gospel requires our individual commitments, as we make those, we become members of faith's chorus.

Dimension 4:
A Daily Bible Journey Plan

Day 1: **Philippians 1:1-14**

Day 2: **Philippians 1:15-26**

Day 3: **Philippians 1:27–2:13**

Day 4: **Philippians 2:14–3:1**

Day 5: **Philippians 3:2-16**

Day 6: **Philippians 3:17–4:7**

Day 7: **Philippians 4:7-23**

All dates in this chronology are approximate, and in some cases even the sequence of events, letters, and travels remain tentative. Question marks indicate points that are especially uncertain by scholars today. Because Paul's authorship of Ephesians, Colossians, and Second Thessalonians is widely questioned by scholars, these letters have been noted in brackets. The Pastoral Epistles (First and Second Timothy and Titus) are not included at all, because so few scholars attribute them to Paul. (As you review the chronology below, you may also find it helpful to refer to the map on the inside back cover of this resource.)

5-10?	Tarsus[?]: birth
30-35?	In Syria[?]: Pharisaic activities, persecution of the church (Galatians 1:13-14)
35-48	Environs of Damascus and Antioch 35 Call to apostleship, time in Arabia (Galatians 1:15-17; 2 Corinthians 11:32-33) 37[?] First visit to Jerusalem (Galatians 1:18-19) 48[?] Second visit to Jerusalem (Galatians 2:1-10)
48-49	In Asia Minor: preaching, establishing churches (Acts 16:1-10)
49-50	In Macedonia (Philippi, Thessalonica, Beroea): preaching, establishing churches (Acts 16:11-17:14)
50-51	In Achaia (Athens, Corinth): preaching, establishing churches (Acts 17:15-18:28) 50, 1 Thessalonians written from Corinth [also 2 Thessalonians?]
51-55	In Ephesus (Acts 19:1-41) 54 1 Corinthians written from Ephesus 55 Brief visit to Corinth? Arrest and imprisonment Philippians and Philemon written from prison
55-56	Return to Macedonia (Acts 20:1) 55 2 Corinthians 1-9 (written from Philippi) 56 2 Corinthians 10-13 and Galatians (written from Thessalonica or Beroea?)
56	Return to Achaia (Acts 20:2-6) Romans written from Corinth Departure for Jerusalem with a collection for the Judean Christians
57-59	In Judea (Acts 21:15-28:15) 58 Delivery of the collection to the Judean Christians 59? Arrest, imprisonment in Caesarea, appeal to the emperor, voyage to Rome
60-62?	In Rome (Acts 28:16-31) [Ephesians and Colossians written from prison?]
62?	Execution

PAUL'S LIFE AND MINISTRY

What we know most certainly about Paul's life and ministry comes from his own letters. The Book of Acts, written several decades after the apostle's death, is more an interpretation of his ministry than a chronicle of it. However Acts, too, is helpful on certain points. Because there are no other ancient sources that provide reliable information about Paul, it is difficult to establish absolute dates for his life and ministry. For an approximation of these, including the tentative dates of his letters, see "Paul's Life and Letters: A Chronology," page 109.

Birth and Upbringing
Paul was born of devout Jewish parents who, according to the Jewish law and tradition, had him circumcised when he was eight days old (Philippians 3:5). There are no references in his letters to either parent, nor to any other family members. However, according to Acts 23:16 he had at least one sister.

Like most Jews in his day, Paul was reared outside Palestine in a Greek cultural environment—apparently in Tarsus (Acts 22:3), which was in Asia Minor (present-day Turkey). As customary in such cases, he had both a Jewish name, "Saul," and one more familiar to Greeks and Romans, "Paul." He probably knew Hebrew (and the related dialect, Aramaic) as well as Greek. In fact, his letters show fluency in Greek and a degree of literary sophistication. This suggests that he was educated, to a fairly high level, in Greek-speaking schools. It is therefore likely that he came from a family of more than average wealth and social standing.

Youth and Pre-Christian Years
We do not know whether Paul had any formal education in the Scriptures and traditions of Judaism. In Acts 22:3 he is identified as having once studied with Gamaliel, a famous Jerusalem teacher of the law. Although Paul writes of having been a Pharisee (Philippians 3:5), we do not know exactly what affiliation with that Jewish sect might have required or provided by way of formal training. We do know, however, that during his years as a Pharisee he had been a persecutor of the church (1 Corinthians 15:9; Philippians 3:6; Galatians 1:13).

The Damascus Experience
Paul's own most important references to his apostolic call are in Galatians 1:1, 11-12, 15-16 and 1 Corinthians 15:8-10. He experienced this as a revelation to him of Jesus Christ as God's Son. (Paul had never known, or even seen Jesus during his earthly ministry.) The author of Acts provides much more detail

110

about Paul's Damascus encounter with Christ (9:1-19; 22:6-16; 26:12-18); the apostle himself writes only about its meaning. It led him to a new understanding of God—as One whose love and salvation embrace the whole of humankind. It also led him to a new understanding of the crucified Jesus—as God's Son who brings freedom from sin, death, and the law, and freedom for new life.

After Damascus

The Earliest Years. Assuming that Paul's Damascus experience occurred about the year 35, there is probably an interval of fifteen years between that life-changing encounter and his earliest surviving letter. He seems to have spent those years mainly in Syria, in the environs of Damascus and Antioch.

During this time Paul reached an understanding with Cephas (Peter) and James, the leaders of the Jerusalem church (Galatians 2:1-10). The Jerusalem apostles would continue to take responsibility for preaching among the Jews, and Paul was free to carry out a mission to the Gentiles. One condition of their agreement was that Paul would collect an offering for Jerusalem from his converts.

The Mission to the Gentiles. The letters that we can attribute with certainty to Paul all date from the period of his missionary activities in Asia Minor, Macedonia, and Achaia (see a map of the journeys of Paul). He succeeded in planting congregations in the Roman province of Galatia and, probably, in the important city of Ephesus. Churches were also established in the Macedonian cities of Philippi and Thessalonica, in the Achaean city of Corinth, and in the nearby seaport community of Cenchreae (see "Paul's Life and Letters: A Chronology," page 109). The apostle kept in touch with his churches by sending special representatives (notably, Timothy and Titus; see "Paul and the Corinthians," page 112) as well as letters. In the end, at least some of his churches did contribute to the collection for Jerusalem (Romans 15:25-27).

The Final Years. After Paul's arrival in Jerusalem with the collection, he was arrested, and then arraigned. During the course of these proceedings he seems to have appealed his case to the Roman emperor, Nero, whereupon he was shipped off to Rome. Although Acts closes with Paul under long-term house arrest in Rome (Acts 28:30-31), tradition says that he was among a sizable number of Christians executed by order of the emperor, perhaps in the year 62.

111

$\mathcal{P}$AUL AND THE CORINTHIANS, A.D. 50-57

Much more is known about Paul's church in Corinth and his dealings with it than about his ministry in any other place. We owe this to the fact that First and Second Corinthians contain many comments about what was going on in the congregation, as well as some references to several visits to Corinth by Paul himself and by others. When the information that can be gleaned from these letters is combined with what can be learned from Paul's other letters and the Book of Acts, it is possible to piece together a plausible, but necessarily tentative, outline of the apostle's Corinthian ministry.

The following overview presupposes that the letter that has come down to us as "Second Corinthians" is in fact a combination of at least two originally separate letters. However, even if this widely held conclusion is rejected, the overall picture remains much the same. Although the dates can only be approximate, the sequence of events is generally secure.

50-51	Paul's first visit to Corinth, and his founding of a church. See 1 Corinthians 1:26–2:5; 2 Corinthians 1:19; Acts 18:1-18.
	Paul's appearance before Gallio, the Roman proconsul in Corinth. See Acts 18:12-17
51-54	Paul's first letter to the Corinthians [lost]. See 1 Corinthians 5:9-11.
54	A letter, along with oral reports, from the Corinthian church to Paul [lost]. See 1 Corinthians 7:1a [the letter]; 1:11; 5:1; 11:18 [some oral reports].
	Paul's dispatch of Timothy to Corinth, from Ephesus. See 1 Corinthians 4:17; 16:10-11.
	Paul's second letter to the Corinthians [our "1 Corinthians"], written from Ephesus. See 1 Corinthians 16:8-9.
55	Timothy's return to Ephesus.
	Paul's second visit to Corinth, unplanned, brief, and "painful." See 2 Corinthians 2:1, 5-8; 7:12.
	Paul's third letter to the Corinthians [lost], from Ephesus. See 2 Corinthians 2:3-4, 9; 7:8-12.
	Paul's dispatch of Titus to Corinth, and subsequent meeting with him in Macedonia. See 2 Corinthians 2:12-13.
	Paul's dispatch of Titus to Corinth for a second time, along with a fourth letter to the Corinthians [our "2 Corinthians," chapters 1–9], from Macedonia. See 2 Corinthians 8:16-22.
56	Paul's fifth letter to the Corinthians [our "2 Corinthians," chapters 10–13], from Macedonia.
	Paul's third visit to Corinth, to pick up the congregation's contribution for the Christians in Jerusalem. See 2 Corinthians 12:14; 13:1-2.
57	Paul's departure from Corinth for Jerusalem. See Romans 15:25-26.

CPSIA information can be obtained at www.ICGtesting.com
Printed in the USA
LVOW07s0703170116

470722LV00004B/8/P